A

VOCABULARY

OF THE

SÁNTÁLI LANGUAGE

A

VOCABULARY

OF THE

SÁNTÁLI LANGUAGE.

BY THE

REV. E. L. Puxley

GYAN

Published by

GYAN

Gyan Publishing House
5, Ansari Road
Daryaganj, New Delhi-110002
Phone: 011-47034999, 9811692060
E-mail: books@gyanbooks.com

Distribution Network
gyanbooks.com
India, USA, Canada, UK, Australia

ISBN: 978-81-212-7067-0 (PB)
First Published, 1868

2nd Impression 2024

Printed at: Gyan Press, Delhi.

A VOCABULARY OF THE SÁNTÁLI LANGUAGE
Author: E. L. PUXLEY

A VOCABULARY OF THE SÁNTÁLI LANGUAGE.

BY THE

REV. E. L. PUXLEY,

LATE MISSIONARY OF THE CHURCH MISSIONARY SOCIETY TO THE SANTALS.

PRINTED BY W. M. WATTS,

80, GRAY'S INN ROAD.

1868.

EXPLANATION.

I.—*Of the letters and diacritical marks used in the Vocabulary.*

In writing Sántáli words I have adopted the system of letters employed by Forbes, Shakespear, and others, for Roman Hindústáni; and as this system is so well known throughout India, it will be only necessary to explain here those marks and points which are peculiar to the present book, and which I have been compelled to adopt for the representation of sounds peculiar to the Sántáli language.

ạ represents a long, gutteral sound, difficult to describe. It is pronounced very nearly as if it were composed of two short separate *a*'s: for instance, the Sántáli word "bạd" might be written "ba-ad," and, is pronounced somewhat like the English "bird" is by people who speak in an affected way, and drop the sound of the *r*.

occurs only after the final vowel of a word, and takes the place of some consonant which has been dropped; while

,, on the other hand, occurs only under the final consonant, which, though not entirely dropped, is very slightly sounded.

These two marks have been sometimes interchanged, *e.g.*, the Sántáli word for "the eye" has been sometimes written "*met*,,", and sometimes "*me:*"; in the one case, the *t* is slightly heard; in the other, it is inaudible. The former (:) represents a peculiar catch, or jerk, on hearing which, one would suppose that the speaker had suddenly stopped to correct himself.

II.—*Of the signs used after the Sántáli words in the Vocabulary.*

† after some words, denotes that the word so marked belongs to some other Indian language.

° denotes that the word is derived from some other Indian language.

? after either a Sántáli or an English word, denotes that I have some doubt as to its correctness.

* occuring after the names of trees, plants, insects, &c., denotes that it is one of a list of such words which I made some years ago; but, as I overlooked this list when revising the manuscript of the Vocabulary, I do not feel certain that the words of it are correctly spelt or correctly translated.*

III.—*Of the forms of Verbs as given in the Vocabulary.*

When possible, the verb has been made to agree with a nominative case of the common gender and third person singular, and the future and past tenses of the neuter and transitive forms have been given. Transitive verbs also are made (when possible) to govern an accusative case of the third person singular and of the common gender, as "*ábo:ái, áp,, enái, kedeái,*" †

Sometimes, however, I have been compelled to depart from this arrangement, for—

* The mention of such words, notwithstanding the doubt attached to them, may be of some service to those who come after me in this field; and therefore I have thought it advisable to insert them.

† In Sántáli a transitive verb agrees, in number, gender, and person, with the word it governs, as well as with the word with which it agrees (or with what we may call its accusative, as well as with its nominative); to effect this agreement two changes occur in the verb, one in the middle, and one at the termination.

Some verbs require that the nominative case with which they agree, and the accusative case which they govern, should either, or both, be in the plural or dual number; and sometimes, again, verbs conjugated as active do not govern an accusative case at all: as "*áchhím kedái*," "he sneezed."

Other verbs can only be conjugated as active, *e.g.*, "*achui eái, achu kedeái.*"

Others, again, are only neuter, as "*aple:ái, aple enái.*"

Sometimes, when such would be its ordinary use, the verb has been put into the dative form, in one or other of the tenses, as "*áchbícho:ái, áchbích enái, ádeái; ájári ái ái, ádeái.*"

Jingling verbs, such as *phás phús, uk buk,* are of very frequent occurrence: for the sake of brevity, I have only repeated the second of these words in the past tenses, as "*akbakáu:ái; bakáu enái.*"

Double verbs (*i.e.*, two verbs formed into, or used as, one) are also common: here I have simply mentioned the root, as the past tenses of such words may be easily discovered, by referring to the latter of the two verbs in its own place.

Occasionally the simple root of a verb, without any tenses, may be met with; the explanation of this is, that not having ever heard of the past tenses of such words, I preferred not to mention anything of which I did not feel tolerably certain.

It should also be remarked, that many transitive verbs, which have been put down in the Vocabulary as forming their perfect tenses in "*ked*" would also require, in speaking, the causal verb *ocho;* as a very slight acquaintance with the language would enable a speaker to put the causal verb in its right place; and, as this is a point more for a Grammar than a Dictionary, I have not thought it necessary to insert it, except when it was absolutely required.

As most verbs may, in Sántáli, be conjugated either as neuter or transitive, I have, in rendering them into English, mixed together the neuter and transitive signification of them; *e.g.*, "*achuro:*," "walk about, move about, repent, restore, bring back."

POSTSCRIPT.

The letters '*n̲r*' are throughout the Vocabulary the representatives of *one* Bengáli letter; the *n* is nasal, and the *r* to be pronounced as if written *ṛ*.

A

Á:, bow

Á: sár, bow and arrow

A:a, ? break down

Ạn, ° law

Abdán, ? master

Abhágiya, † luckless, unfortunate

Abhrá:, lake, water, piece of water

Ábo:ái, *áp„ enái*, *kedeái*, alight, wash the face

Abolá, ° beast, dumb animal

Aboṛ bodhaí eái, *kedeái*, flatter, wheedle

Ábuko:ái, *ábuk enái*, *kedeái*, wash the hands

Achár bichár, conduct, life, walk and conversation

Áchbícho:ái, *áchbích enái*, *ádeái*, despise, scorn, loathe, hate, turn from in disgust

Áchel páchel, wealth, splendour, grandeur

Áchhímo:ái, *áchhím enái*, *kedái*, sneeze

Achká:ái, *achká enái*, *kedeái*, surprise, startle, not to expect

Achkáte, *achkági*, suddenly, unexpectedly, accidentally

Achkámaṛ, sudden

Achráu, to sow a field with rice to be afterwards transplanted

Achui eai, *achu kedeái*, engage labourers, employ, give employment

Achuro:ái, *achur enái*, *kedeái*, walk about or round, move about, repeat, bring back, restore, answer

Achur ruaṛ, reward, repay, revenge

Ạd, the beginning

Ạd chalí, original custom, old tradition

Ạd khoná:, from eternity

Ádo:ái, át,, enái, kedeaí, lose, forfeit, mistake, lose the way

Ádá, a measure (about seven bushels)

Áḍá, a shelter for cattle from the mid-day sun, a shed

Ádá: á, ádái ená, ádá kedái, to be seasoned (with salt, &c.), rub in (oil, &c.)

Ádá báṛi, tend silkworms

Ádáingn ái, ádáing kedái, gain, make a profit

Ádár, lust, heat (of animals)

Áḍepáse, neighbouring, near

Áḍepáserenko, neighbours

Áder eái, kedeái, shew hospitality, take in, admit

Aḍger, to go

Ádh,? dear, costly

Ádhá gnindá, midnight

Ádhán, some, a little, half

Ádhár, fodder, provision

Ádh baisure,° at half age, prematurely

Ádhi:á, ádhi ená, kedeái, lessen, diminish, abate

Adherom,° irreligious, wicked

Adhua, without the Sántál marks on the left arm

Aḍi, much, many, very

Aḍigárte, noisily, fast, violently, loudly, strongly

Aḍi uṭar, very many, abundant

Aḍi baṛi:, very much

Aḍi okoi:, a good deal

Aḍi chhoṭ } often
Aḍi dháu }

Aḍi aḍi } many kinds
Aḍi tirit }

Ádo, and, moreover [urine

Aḍo jòng, make water, pass

Ádom, some, a little, a few

Ádop,, influence, effect, intention

Aduá, rice eaten without boiling

Áedári, inheritance, possession, authority

Afsor,° means, opportunity

Afsoro:, obtain opportunity

Agílo: á, agíl ená, kedái, load a cart too heavy in front

Agnui, to give to drink, gild, cover (with gold, &c.)

Agui eái, agu kedeái, bring, fetch, take (life)

Agu daṛái, bring, come bringing

Agu oṭo, restore

Agu ocho, send for

Ahá, alas!

Ahá:ái, ahái enái, ahá kedái, be bewitched. [It is thought that when one who has eaten filth in his childhood looks on another eating, he vomits]

Ahakáu:ái, ahakáu enái, kedái, pant

Áhár, a dam, bank

Áhaṛí, tender of silkworms

Ahináu:á, ahináu enái, kedái, commence to rot, begin to corrupt or spoil

Aho, no, not

Ahongkár,° pride

Ái:, ái: gi, own, himself

Ái:á, ái ená, kedái, guess, measure, ascertain

Áikáu:ái, áikáu ená, kedeái, grope in the dark, guess, perceive, taste, experience, feel, seem, appear

Áikáu ṭhík, discover, settle

Áikáu gelá, test, try

Ạil mạilte, disorderly

Ạil mạilo: á, ạil mạil ená, kedeái, confuse, put into confusion, disorder

Áimá, much, many

Áimái, woman

Ainomo: á, ainom enái, kedeái, paint round the eyes, apply 'ainom' to the eyes

Áiomán, ? select, appropriate

Ájár, ? ill, sick, diseased

Ájári ái ái, ádeái, call on, visit, have an interview with

Ajátiya,° outcast

Ajauṛi, empty

Ájbíjá:, ájbiá:, right, proper, due

Ajhánṭo:ái, ajhánṭ enái, kedeái, use force, be violent

Ajo áiái, ádeái, feed (another), nurse

Akái ái, aká kedeái, suspend, hang up

Akál, † famine, scarcity

Akáuná, a shrub ?

Akbakáu:ái, bakáu enái, kedeái, discomfit, set in confusion, be in trouble, pant, suffer from heat

Akhạini, pitchfork, forked stick

Akhírre,° finally, lastly, afterwards

Ákil,° wise, learned

Ákil bud,° wisdom, knowledge

Akkáji, to swear, take an oath

Ákote, by their own accord

Ákringno:á, ákringn ená, ákring kedái, sell, dispose of

Ákudo: á, ákut„ enái, kedeái, be quick, hasten, be in a fuss

Ákut„ bákut„, difficult (used of a stony, thorny, hilly road)

Alái áiái, enái, alá kedeái, surrender, give over or up, put for a prize

Áláng, the tongue

Alát,, olodo:ái, olot,, enái, kedeái, be confused in talking, contradict one's self

Aláundhá, dazzled, scarcely seeing (as one coming into a strong light)

Álbudahá, *Áldhundhahá*, senseless, animal-like, beastly

Álgá, easy, convenient

Álgáte, easily

Alo, not (with imperative and subjunctive moods)

Amáli eái, enái, kedeái,° give authority to

Ambá: ambogo:ái, ambo: enái, kedeái, roll from side to side, waddle like a drunkard

Ámdá, a division of the country [the part of the country which a man knows well is his 'ámdá']

Amdáj ái, kedái, ° guess

Ámlá, † court officers

Ámlá kaplá, ditto

Ám míká dar, five-leaved mango branch, with which the jog manjhi sprinkles the young couple at weddings

Aṇ,° law (see also *ąąn*)

Anąri,° stranger

Anbhul, unconscious, out of senses

Anchár,° hem, edge of dress, fringe, border of dress

Ancháu,? to offer sacrifice, present in sacrifice

Andá: tawágo:ái, tawá: enái, kedeái, go astray, be missing, not to find, discomfit, confound

Anḍár onḍoro:ái, ondor enái, kedeái, be confused, lose the way, be caught in a storm, be astonished, stare, open the eyes in astonishment

Andhá eái, andhái enái, andhá kedeai, deal deceitfully, delude

Andhá dhund eái, kedeái, oppress, make great disturbance

Anḍíá, bull, male

Anḍijo:ái, anḍi: enai, kedeái, deceive, coax, wheedle, seduce, inveigle, defraud

Ándmándáu:ái, mándáu enái, kedeái, be troubled, perplexed

Andoro: á, andor ená, kedái, sound, report, make a row, make noise

Andrá, half blind, having dull eyes

Andu: mandu: frightened, startled, looking all round

Ané: dhánejo:ai, dháne: enai, kedeai, have plenty, be wealthy, affluent, have abundance

Angáu:ái, angáu enai, kedái, admit, confess

Angeno:, to disappear for ever in a haunted tank

Angíro:ái, angír enái, kedeái, elope with (a girl), carry off (a woman)

Angoicho:ái, angoich enái, kedái, admit, confess

Angop,, angobo:ái, angop,, enái, kedái, gasp as a dying person, sigh, yawn

Angrop, a jacket, "kurta"

Ani: with (in compos) as *búdáni:* wise, *úpáni:* hairy

Anjedo:á, anjet,, enái, kedái, dry up (as a river)

Anjle:ái, anjle enái, kedái, hold the hands open to catch something

Anjomo: á, anjom enái, kedeái, ádeái, hear, listen, grant, obey, address, accede

Anjom orom, know or understand from hearing

Áṉrgátre, early, before the usual time (supposing that something is to be done afterwards)

Áṉrgo:ái, *Áṉrgunái* } *Áṉrgoi enái, áṉrgo kedeái*, descend, take down

Áṉrgom, harrow (a flat and long piece of wood used in breaking the clods of newly-ploughed fields)

Áṉrkus kathá, stirring up, reproach, words of chiding

Áṉrti áiái, ádeái, help a second time to food

Ansái ái, ansá kedái, make a noise

Ánṭ, hard, difficult, requiring force, loud

Ánṭhoe, a storm, strong wind

Ánṭo:ái, ánṭ enái, kedái, do something quickly, or strongly

Anṭáu: á, anṭáu ená, kedeái, suffice, be contained, divide? hold out

Aṇwṭhá, a ring for the great toe

Apábaria: áko, bará enáko, ket koái, separate, divide, part asunder

Apájo: ákin, apáj enákin, concede precedence, respect

Ápán ápín,° mutual, several, respective

Ápán ápíno: ákin, ápín enákin, ket koái, assume different sides, mutually separate

Apạri, arrow-head

Áphím,†, opium

Aphṭau: ákin, aphṭáu enákin, ket koái, challenge, provoke

Ápiro:á, ápir ená, kedái, fly off obliquely

Aple:ai, aple enái, climb a smooth tree by legs and arms

Apná apní, mutual, several, respective

Áp,,napáio: wash clean (the face)

Apnár,° own (my own, thy own, &c., according to the nom. of the verb)

Ápuing, ápum, ápát,,, my, thy, his father

Ár, and, also, again, other

Árhoṇ, again, also, more, other, moreover

Árá, red

Árá upál, the red lily

Ảṛá:, greens, potatoes [tables

Áṛá:sákám, greens, vege-

Áṛágái, áṛá: enái, kedeái, free, set at liberty, escape, leave, loosen, abate, discharge, let-off gun, &c.

Áṛáng, voice, sound

Aṛáni, * a measure so called

Árá̱ṉr, a yoke

Árdá, unploughed (ground) fresh

Áṛe, edge

Áṛerenko, neighbours

Árejo: á, áre: ená, kedái, water (by baling up the water in hands or in a "*chiṭai*")

Árel, hailstone

Aṛi:, ? rice-field in ridges

Ari ái, kedái, ordain, appoint

Áríd aí, árit,, kedái, look aslant, watch another stealthily

Arik parik, very cleanly

Áṛing ái, áṛiṇ kedái, strain off water from cooked rice

Áríso:ái, árís enái, kedeái, scream,? make a noise,? be vexed, bothered, tired, give offence

Arján, populous, cultivated

Arján eái, enái, kedeái, goad, spur, spear

Arjáu: á, arjáu ená, kedái, gain, make profit

Aṛjháu: á, aṛjháu ená, kedeái, be entangled, run against, entrap [plain

Arji ái, kedái,° request, com-

Arojo:ái, aroj kedái,° make an application, beg, beseech

Árpá, a fathom, the stretch of the arms, the bundle of rice paid for cutting it

Arṛáu:ái, arṛáu enái, kedái, bellow (as a buffalo), roar

Arsí, glass, mirror

Árubo:ái, árup,, ená, kedeái, wash (rice, &c.), wash away, (as by a flood)

Árup,, safhá } wash clean
Árup,, pond }

Ás,† hope, desire, trust

Áso:ái, ás enái, kedeái, hope, trust, encourage, take refuge

Ás chhuṭáu:, be disappointed, despair

Asambher, illimitable

Ásámí, defendent, borrower, client

Ásen eái, kedeái, tend (a child, &c.), carry about, lead about

Áse: táse:, plentiful, very rich, luxuriant

Asírbád,† blessing

Asírbád em, bless

Áshandaní, crying greatly, peevish (a child)

Ásket,° lazy

Ásol,° chief, principal

Áso khái: te, especially

Ásrá:ái, ásrái enái, ásrá kedeái,† hope, trust, animate, encourage

Assis,† curse

Asukh,† discomfort, disquiet

Asúlo:ái, asúl enái, kedeái, support, nourish, take care of, nurse

Asúl hopon, adopted son

Ásúr, glutton

Aswári,° cavalry, rider

Atái ai, ená, atá kedeái, fry, parch, bake

Áṭál, layer, row

Áṭál sákám, leaves of a book

Bár áṭál, twofold, doubled

*Áṭál bahá,** kind of flower

Átángo :á, átáng kedái, take, catch (in hands or vessel), take something into open hand, put hand under (something to support it)

Átáro: á, átár enái, kedeái, set on fire, burn jungle

Áṭedo: á, áṭet,, ená, kedái, spread out (*e.g.* sheet, &c.)

Áṭet,, á:, bed-clothes

Aten ái, kedái, listen, hear secretly, bend the ear (to listen)

Athán dá:, a flood (from overflowing of rivers), very deep water

*Athel,** a kind of tree 'athela'

Aṭhreno: á, áṭhren enái, kedeái, prop up the body, support from beneath

Áting, to feed (as cattle), graze

Aṭkáro:ái, aṭkár enái, kedeái, prove, try, test, feel

Aṭkáu: á, aṭkáu enái, kedeái,[o] obstruct, hinder, prevent

Áṭhir eái, kedeái, carry off

Áṭkuṛá, sonless, heirless

Áṭkuṭí, thistles

Átmá,† spirit, soul

Átná, a kind of tree

Áto, village, hamlet

Átrá: á, átrái enái, átrá kedeái, miss, fail to obtain, fail to reach

Atruingno:ái, atruingn enái atruing kedeái, be dissatisfied, dislike

Átu, flood

Átu:ái, átui ená, átu kedái, float, flow, run (as water)

Átu: gaḍá, bed of river

Aturo:ái, atur enái, kedeái, trail along

Aṭwár din,[o] Sunday

Audá, meditation, intention

Audá jong, be prudent, far-seeing

Auṇsá bauṇsá, race, lineage, descendants

Auri, soon, before, not yet

Auṛiá, uselessly, falsely, causelessly, idly, in vain

Ausáno:ái, ausán enái, kedeái, obtain ease, rest, lighten, alleviate, mitigate, recover, assist

Aután, fort,? concealed spot, safe retreat, strong place suitable for fighting in

Awátappá:ái, tappái enái, tappá kedeái, be in distress

Áyám bing, a snake, the cobra

Ayogi, hallo! indeed! O my! dear me!

Áyup, evening

Áyup payár, evening

B

Bá, no, not, (in compos, as *báing, bám, bái*, &c.)

Báng, no, not

Báb ái, ádeái, order, petition, request, speak

Bábádo:, bábát,, enái, have the itch

Bábái á:, case (in which to keep things)

Bábár, by two's, two and two

Báber, rope

Bábu, term used in addressing an inferior or younger person

Bábur,† a thorney tree like mimosá

Bachhá,[o] bull calf

Bachhi, heifer

Bachháu:ái, bachháu enái, kedeai, pick out, select, choose

Bachháu tod,,, select (out of many)

Bachkạr, harlot, prostitute, courtezan (a caste)

Báchkom, grass rope, coarse grass, used for beds, chairs, &c.

Bachláu:ái, bachláu enái, kedeái, preserve, defend, be safe, save, escape

Bád, bádí, accuser, enemy, opponent, hatred

Bạd ái, kedeái, cultivate

Bạd, a plain-like field

Baḍạị, boastful, arrogant; pride, vainglory, conceit

Badáṇw, badisti, enmity, ill-feeling, ill-wishing

Baḍáio: á, baḍái enái, kedeái, appear, be known

Báde háláng, draw out warp in weaving

Badhá, wooden sandals

Khunṭi badhá, high ditto

*Bạḍháu: á, bạḍháu enái, kedeái,*⁰ promote, increase

Badhí: á, badhí enái, kedeái, bind up, wind up, wrap up

Badhistí, rival

*Baḍhohí,*⁰ carpenter, mason

Badot, evil

*Bagáhí,*⁰ tiger which has killed many people

Bagdáu: á, bagdáu enái, kedeái, miss, fail, forget something, lose the way

*Bághin,** thorn bush

Bagí: á, bagí enái, kedeái, quit, abandon, forsake, leave

Bágwán, garden of mangoes

Bahá, flower

Bahá: a, bahái enái, kedeái, flower, bloom, adorn with flowers

Bahá din, festival

Bahá kochá, flower-garden

Bahá gutui, to weave a garland

Bahá saṇwhá, to marry a second time

*Bahálo:ái, bahál enái, kedeái,*⁰ be appointed, restored to one's position

Báhaná: gnutum, surname, nickname, the name by which an individual is usually known, though not his original one

Baháu:ái, baháu enái, kedeái, live, exist, last, support

*Bahire,*⁰ external, outer

Bahire se:, outside

*Bahní,*⁰ whirlpool

Bahú, wife, bride, daughter-in-law

Bahú áiái, kedeái } to marry a wife
Bahú agui }

Bạị,? age

Bái ái, kedeái, take care of, keep, preserve safely

Bai baite, softly, gently

Bainá,[o] advances of money

Bạio: ái, bại enái,† be delirious, be sick of "bai"

Bairi,† enemy

Baisáu: á, baisáu enái, kedeái, lend on usury, fix, appoint, settle, let out, hire out, establish, be firm

Bájár,[o] bazaar, market, city, town

Bajáu:ái, bajáu enái, kedeái, hit against, receive a blow, knock or strike against (*e. g.* wind), come in contact with, affect (*e. g.* sickness)

Bají:ái, bají enái, kedeái, turn a summersault

Bájú, armlet, brass or tin ornaments or charms, worn on the arm

Bák,† crane

Bákát, bukudo:ái, bukut,, enái, kedeái, quicken (as fœtus in the womb)

Bakáu:ái, bakáu enái, kedeái, inspire, put into the mind, speak thoughtlessly, let something slip out of the mouth

Bakhanáu:ái, bakhanáu enái, kedeái, give obscene abuse

Bákhen̲r ái, ádeái, pray (to Satan) invoke

Bakher } a double house with enclosure between, house and garden, court, establishment
Bakhol }

Bakhoro:ái, bakhor kedái, transplant

Bákí,† remainder

Bák junú, firefly

Báklá:, bark, peel, rind

Baksís,[o] gift, present, favour

Bákyá, trumpet

Bálá erá,* son's wife's mother, daughter's husband's mother

Bálbaláu:ái, bálbaláu enái, sweat, perspire

Bále, young, tender, delicate

Bále gidirá, young child, baby

Bále dábi, gristle at the end of collar-bone, cartilege

Bále molo, new moon

Balidán,† offerings, sacrifice

Bálo: á, bál enái, kedeái, open (a boil, &c.), make a hole with red-hot iron

Bámber, torch

Bambkáu: á, bambkáu ená, kindle, blaze up

Báná, a bear; a kind of bird

Báná:, bush-hook

Bánám, kind of banjo made of wood, with one string

Bánám ái, kedái, play the "bánám"

Bánár, both

Bánár se:, in both directions, on either hand

Bánátok,* a kind of tree

Bánbasi, deluge, flood

Bancháu:ái, bancháu enái,° *kedeái*, live, survive, preserve, defend, save

Bánd,° bank, embankment

Bánd tol, to raise a bank

Bándá, birdlime, the tree from which birdlime is extracted

Bánde:ái, bánde enái, kedeái, put on clothes (woman), dress (woman)

Bándhok,† pledge, token

Bándhono:ái, bándhon enái, kedeái, fascinate, charm, bind with securities, take security

Bándí, large straw-rope baskets in which "dhán" is kept

Banḍíá, bull with short tail

Bándo narí, wild vine, a creeper

Bandpará,* a snake that crawls either way

Bandúk,† gun

Báng, no, not

Bángmá, viz., that is, i.e.

Bángkhán, unless, otherwise, or else, even

Báng ákil, stupid

Báng jo, barren, fruitless

Báng bororá, not clean (as half-washed clothes)

Báng muchạt,, endless, eternal

Báng goju: i:, immortal

Báng dosi:, innocent

Báng patiáu, to disbelieve

Báng gáno:, be impossible

Báng táhen, be absent

Báng dayái: cruel, unmerciful, inexorable, unrelenting

Báng khusí / *saná* } dislike, be dissatisfied

Báng jurí: / *mído:* / *tulujo:* / *gnápámo:* } disagree

Báng disạị, be delirious, be out of one's senses

Báng gog,,, deny

Báng reben, decline

Báng hilo:,? uncultivated

Bang lángá:, be indefatigable

Báng lájáu:, be shameless

Báng bichạr, be thoughtless

Báng dáṛe, be unable

Báng hopon áni: hopono: i: } barren (animals), childless

Bangáurá, cotton-seed

Bạṇh áiái, ádeái, stir-up, excite

Bánjhí,° barren (woman)

Bánká, bent, curved

Bankí, anklet

Bánṟiá,* "kohndá" a kind of pumpkin

Bánṟsi,† fishhook

Bánu:, is not, not to exist, (only in present tense)

Banwáṭo: á, banwáṭ ená, kedái, to return to jungle again

Banyá†, trader

Báoṉre, reel of cotton, two sticks like a V

Bápágo: ákin, bápá: enákin, ketkinái, separate, part (as man and wife), break-off friendship

Bápháu: á, báphán ena, kedái,° boil, steam

Báplá, marriage, wedding

Báplá: ákin, báplá enákin, marry

Bápuṛi:, poor, wretched, miserable

Bár, two

Bár jíwí ákán, pregnant

Bár mochá, two-faced, hypocritical

Bár mon, deceitful, changeable, fickle

Bár pạilá, a measure about a quart

Barábar,†even, equal, uniform, level

Barábariren, mediator, umpire, one who stands between

Báráhí, thick rope

Baṛáio: á, baṛái kedái, appear, be known, know, understand, suppose, think (see also *baḍáio:*)

Bárduṉruṇi:, bat, flying fox

Báṛe, banyan tree

Báreto:ái, báret enái,' *kedeái*, accompany the bride to her husband's village or house

Báṛgi, field, garden

Baṛháu,[o] increase (see *baḍháu*)

Baṛi:, bad, evil, wicked, sinful, injury, defect

Baṛi: kamí, misconduct, fault

Baṛi: kamí hoṛ / *Baṛi: i:* — misconducted, an evil person

Baṛíjo:ái, baṛi: enái, kedeái, injure, be guilty, corrupt, destroy

Baṛi: men, to abuse, slander

Bariạt,[o] wedding guests, wife's brothers

Bárkáite, dissembling, mockingly

Bárki, sheet, "dohar"

Báro hoṛo, early rice

Bár phúl,* a white flower

Bárte ái, kedái, notify a hunt, publish

Baṛtí, more

Bárti ái, ádeái, give generously (with both hands)

Baru,* oil tree

Baruḍáng, toad, large frog

Bạs, age

Básángo: á, básáng enái, kedái, heat (water), warm (water)

Báske daká,[o] rice kept from the preceding day

Báskiá jom, break fast

Báskiá ber / *Básiám ber* — about nine o'clock

Báso: á, bás enái, kedeái, emit odour, smell badly, stink

Básudo:ai, básut„ enái, ádeái, regard highly, reverence, respect, think well of

Baṭá: baṭágo:ái, baṭá: enái, kedeái, writhe (as a dying person)

Batáu ái, kedái, acknowledge, confess, obey, regard

Baṭí, cup

Bát katáu,[o] disprove, disobey, stop (another) in speaking

Batláu áiái, ádeái,[o] teach, show

Baṭrí, toe ornament (three rings which produce a jingling)

Battí,† lamp

Báuláu:ái, báuláu enái, rave, become insane, be very drunk, very angry

Baunṛá,† stumpy, sturdy, a a dwarf

Báuṇsá,[o] race, lineage, descendents

Báyábán, inundation, flood

Báyár, male buffalo, bull

Beáj,† interest on money

Bebenáui:, be: náui:, creator, maker

Bebhorsá,[o] disappointed
Beḍá, field, low land near river
Beḍaul,† shapeless
Bedhá, crabbed, knotty
Beḍhái, *beṛhái*, all round, on all sides
Bedháu:ái, *bedháu enái*, *kedeái*, wind round, wrap round
Bedisá, careless, thoughtless
Bedo:ái, *bet" enái*, *kedeái*, hoodwink, blindfold, cover the face or mouth
Befáida,† in vain, useless, fruitless
Begár,[o] separately, apart, asunder
Begáro: á, *begár enái*, *kedeái*, separate, set apart
Begár idí, carry off by force
Begár begár, distinguish between
Begor,[o] except, unless, without
Behál,[o] astonishing, extraordinary
Behudís, thoughtless
Beíá, causeless, useless
Bejhá, target
Bejhái ái, *bejhá kedái*, aim at
Bejo:ái, *be:kedái*, vomit
Bekám,[o] useless, causeless, idle
Belá,[o] time
Belá machhá, proper season

Bele, egg
Bele ái, *kedái*, lay eggs
Bele:, ripe
Bele: á, *bele ená*, *kedái*, ripen
Belkeng,? leaf, letter
Belo: á, *bel ená*, *kedái*, establish, [set up
Belogo: á, *belog" ená*, *kedeái*, give way
Belteng, very small
Belteng galái, a collection of small insects
Bená,* kind of grass
Benáhak,[o] useless, causeless
Benáu ái, *kedeái*,[o] make, create, form
Beṇḍáu: á, *beṇḍáu enái*, *kedeái*, kill, destroy, perish
Beneá, adversary, enemy
Benged ái, *benget" kedeái*, gaze, stare, spy, watch, be kind to, pity, help
Benget" ruaṛo:, look back
Benget" phariạ, have one's eyesight restored
Bepenged, stare mutually, mutually spy, squint at each other
Beṉrbágo:ái, *beṉrbá: enái*, *kedeái*, stammer, lisp, stutter
Beṇt,† cane, ratan
Bentáro:ái, *bentár enai*, *kedeái*, tie on (clothes, &c.)

Ber, berá,[o] season, time

Ber hásuro:, set (as sun)

Ber rákáb, rise (as sun)

Ber he ber, seasonably

Berá berí, staring round (in anger), angrily stamping about

Beredái, beret,, enái, kedeái, lift up, raise, awake, be or make well

Beret,, ruaṛo, rise again, recover

Berel, raw, uncooked, cold (water)

Berelo: á, berel enái, kedeái, live, dwell

Bergá, dwarf (used in anger)

Beṛhái se:, all round, on all sides. See also *bedhái*

Berhon, daily wages

Berthá,[o] impossible, in vain

Bes,† right, good, better, proper

Beso: á, bes enái, kedeái, to be or make good

Bes okoi:te, well, properly

Besáu eái, kedeái, mock, mimic

Beshorom, besrom,[o] shameless, bold, forward

Besímạ,[o] boundless

Besoṇk, breathless

Besorá,* a bird so called (of prey)

Bethá, disease of the liver, soreness of the whole body, especially on loins

Beṭhikána,† careless, thoughtless, uncertain, in the dark

Bhábná, affliction, sorrow

Bhábná:ái, bhábná enái, kedeái, be afflicted, be concerned, feel anxious, be dejected

Bhachkáu:ái, bhachkáu enái kedeái, rave, chatter

Bhádeso:ái, bhádes enái kedeái, use irony, ridicule, sneer, despise, revile, slander, abuse, deceive, make pretences

Bhádo:ái, bhát,, enái, kedeái, be satisfied, have a belly full

Bhádu,* a kind of tree so called

Bhagáu:ái, bhagáu enái, kedeái,[o] overcome, put to flight

Bhági, good, well, excellent, proper

Bhági sabit,te }
Bhági lekáte } properly, well
Bhági sahiṇtte }

Bhagnái, sister's son

Bhagwá:ái, bhagwái enái, bhagwá kedeái, wear the "nangoti"

Bháincháing (*m-t*) my (thy, his) elder brother's son

Bhájún, pot, pitcher, vessel

Bhákhá,† language, spoken dialect

Bhalá,† just! well then!

Bhálogo:ái, *bhálo: enái*, *kedeái*, be mad, insane, rabid

Bhálo: setá, mad dog

Bhalwá, a swallow (bird)

Bhándán, ceremonies of purification after death of a friend

Bhandár,† granary, storehouse

Bhanduro:ái, *bhandur enái*, *kedeái*, to undress (as a woman whose *sárhi* has fallen)

Bhandur ái, *kedái*, waste time, remain idle

Bháng,† hemp for smoking

Bhángáto: á, *bhángát ená*, *kedái*, be ruined, abandoned (as a field with broken banks)

Bhangalá bháto: be destroyed, be desolate

Bhangwá, idle

Bhanjáu:ái, *bhanjáu enái*, *kedeái*,⁰ exercise the body, change money

Bhanktáu:á, *bhanktáu enái*, *kedeái*, set astray, deceive

Bháo,† rate, price

Bhaontiá,* an antelope of that name

Bhárá,† fare, rent, tax

Bhárábháto:á, *bhát enái*, *kedeái*, die, sustain loss, perish, spend in vain

Bharando, whirlwind

Bharánring, bee

Bharí, employment, work for labourers, wages, food

Bharí,⁰ difficult, heavy

Bharí hormo, pregnant

Bharí: á, *bharí enái*, *kedeái*, load (a cart, &c.)

Bháriа ái, *kedái*, carry on the shoulder

Bháro:ai, *bhároi enái*, *bháro kedeái*, be astonished, be amazed, wonder

Bhartí: á, *bhartí enái*, *kedeái*,† be pregnant, be admitted, be filled

Bharunro:ái, *bharunr enái*, *kedeái*, unravel, become loose, become thin (*e.g.* rope)

Bhasí:ái, *bhasí enái*, *kedeái*, form habits, become accustomed to

Bhatáu:á, *bhatáu ená*, *kedái*, fill up, level

Bháti,? bellows

Bhaunrá:á, *bhaunrái ená*, *bhaunrá kedái*, bore a hole (with gimlet, &c.)

Bhayádi,⁰ family, relations

Bhed,† gist, secret, meaning, essence

*Bheḍá, bheḍí,** ram, ewe

Bhejá,† subscription, collection

Bhejá kouḍi, ditto

Bhekbheko:ái, bhek enái, kedeái, chatter, talk much, repeat over and over

Bhembhá, foolish, ignorant

Bhen, to mourn, weep, wail for the dead

Bheoná, a vision

Bhibiko:ái, bhibik enái, kedeái, be indignant

Bhíjáu: á, bhíjáu ená, kedeái, operate (medicine), influence, have effect upon, overcome (sorrow, &c.)

Bhiná: á, bhiná enái, kedeái, separate, distinguish

Bhingṛáu: áko, bhingṛáu enáko, kethoái, break-up (an assembly), abandon (purpose)

Bhiṛáu, to cleave, stick

*Bhiri jáe,** a kind of grass

Bhiriko:ái, bhirik enái kedeái, start back, be disgusted, dislike

Bhiṛkáu:ái, bhirháu enái, kedeái, frighten, startle, surprise, terrify (see also *biṛkáu*)

Bhít,† wall

Bhítrí,° inside, inner

Bhítríte, within

Bhochbhocháu:ái, bhocháu enái, kedeái, chatter, scold, talk incoherently

Bhodor, unrepaired, abandoned; to fail, abandon

Bhog ái, bho: kedái, bark (as a dog)

Bhogáu:ái, bhogáu enái, kedeái, be corpulent

Bhogoj, bhoj,† feast

Bhoj ái, kedái, feast

Bhokhár,† sheath of sword

Bhokráu ái, kedái, low (as a cow, &c.)

Bhor, blessing, favour

Bhoráu: á, bhoráu ená, kedái,° fill up, close up

Bhorok, idea, conception, sudden thought

Bhorsá:ái, bhorsái enái, bhorsá kedeái,° trust, hope, encourage, comfort

Bhorsá em, encourage

Bhoṭogo: a, bhoṭo: ená, blow (as flowers), bud

Bhoṭro, blunt

Bhoyono:ái, bhoyon enái, kedeái, fear

Bhu:, hole

Bhuchung, ignorant, stupid, dull

Bhuga:, hole, cave of animals

Bhugago: á, bhuga: ená, kedái, break through or down, make a hole, pierce

Bhukú, white ant

Bhuláu:ái, bhuláu enái, kedeái,° lead astray

Bhulkáu: á, bhulkáu ená, kedái, spring up (fountain), ooze up, gush out, swell (river)

Bhumbuk, fountain, strong spring

Bhumbuko: á, bhumbuk ená, kedái, spring out (with force), gush forth,

Bhungráu: á, bhungráu enái, kedeái, cut into blocks

Bhunjáu:ái, bhunjáu enái, kedeái, bear, endure, support, pass (time), live

Bhurago:á, bhura: ená, kedái, fill (a vessel by sinking it)

Bhuri:ái, bhurí enái, kedeái, take off (women's clothes)

Bhurujo:ái, bhurui: enái, kedeái take off (men's clothes)

Bhurká, morning star

Bhurní, small holes in houses for the smoke to escape by; wooden latch of the door

Bhusku eái, kedeái, provoke, irritate

Bhút,† demon, evil spirit

Bi:ái, bi enái, kedeái, be satisfied, full

Bibák, all, the whole

Bibhorom, bibostor, naked

Bichar,° judgment, thought

Bi:chari:, judge

Bichárá, good man, generous

Bichhiá, toe ornament

Bichhláu, to sprain, be lame

Bichkát, hatred

Bida:ái, bida enái, kedeái,° dismiss, depart, take leave

Bídal, generation

Bídáu eái, kedái, tempt, try, test, examine

Biddáp, to crawl, walk

Bidesiá odoko:, go to travel

Bidhuá, bastard

Bidlaio: áko, bidlai enáko, hetkoái, scatter in all directions

Bído: á, bít,, ená, kedeái, bury, embed, insert

Bidráu, to excite mutiny, get up a strike, wander away, migrate

Bidrá bidri:ái, bidri enái, kedeái, wander about, be a vagabond

Bidyá,† knowledge, learning, sorcery; a game so called

Bíghá,† a measure (about one acre)

Bígháí ái, bíghá kedái, measure land

Bigṛá bigṛí,° to confound, confuse

Bijlí,† lightning

Bikol,° uneasy, anxious

Bilạn, bilạt, an enclosed plain free from jungle

Bilbiláu:ái, bilbiláu enái, kedeái, inspire fear, terrify

*Bili: bálángo: á, báláng ená, kedái,*brandish, glisten, clean clothes

Bilombo:ái, bilomb enái, kedeái,† tarry, delay

Bilṭáu:á, bilṭáu enái, kedeái, slip away, lose, disappear, mislead, misplace

Bin, without

Bin onmánte, thoughtlessly, heedlessly

Bin botorte, fearlessly

*Bin phasiạráte,*unfeignedly

Bin kahán̲ kahin̲, causelessly [less

Bin hor, pathless, track-

Bin muchạt, boundless

Bín sulúk, unfriendliness

Bin ghaṭí, sinless, faultless, innocent

Bin dagá, spotless

Binḍạ, bundle of grass, &c.

Bindạṛo: á, bindạṛ enái, kedeái, cast down, turn over, lie flat, fall, overthrow

Bindhaṛ, a wooden fence

Bindi gáná:, cobweb

Bindṛángo:ái, bindṛáng enái, kedeái, slip, fall, sprawl

Binḍujo:ái, binḍui: ádeái, sneer at, despise, curl the lip in scorn

Bing, serpent, snake

Bini, fan (to blow the fire with) [tables

Binṭhí, curved knife for vege-

Binti ái, ádẹái,† proclaim, beseech, request, preach, say grace, entreat

Bio:ái (see *bi*)

Bipot,† loss, misfortune, affliction, injury

Bir, jungle, forest

Bir pakáṛ, very dense jungle

Birbáu, hurricane, tempest, storm

Bir hoṛ, wild man, a tribe so called, Sántál gipsies

Bir jánwar, wild beast

Biṛí hoṛ,° convict, prisoner

Biṛkáu (see *bhiṛkáu*)

Birot,? without understanding

Bis,† poison

Bisbakháno:ái, bakhán kedeái, abuse

Bisi, backbone

Bisi muṭí,? unremitting, urgent, diligent

Bisphoṛá,† abscess, boil

Bispíta,? annoyance

Bíṭạ,° span

Biṭhí, employment for food, work, food for wages

Bitkil, cow (female buffalo)

Biṭolo:ái, bíṭol enái, kedeái, lose caste, put out of caste

Bochor,° year (used with a numeral)

Boḍá,* a kind of reptile, brown snake

Bodá, ram

Bodám,? image

Boḍe, muddy, dirty, slime

Boḍe losot, thin mud

Bodháu eái, kedeái, play to a child, quiet a child

Bodlá, bodol,° change

Bodolo: á, bodol enái, kedeái, change, exchange

Bodol hatáu, take vengeance, revenge

Bodol achur, repay, reward

Bodolte, instead of

Bodnám ochoi,° disgrace, dishonour

Boḍojo:á, boḍoi: ená, kedái, wring out

Boho:, head

Boho: khaprí, skull

Boho: rukui, to strike the head

Boho: kebe: kebe:, shaking of the head, palsy

Bohogeái, boho: enái, kedeái, make a head, put a head on, speak of, abuse

Bohor bohor, glutinous, viscous, sticky, thick like jelly

Boihá,° brother, relative

Bọjhá,† load, weight

Bojo: á, boi: ená, kedái, draw out, draw sword, drag out, take off (clothes)

Boká:, plate made of half a pumpkin

Bokhár,† sheath of sword

Boko, the heart

Boko ing, m, t, my, thy, his, younger brother

Bokom bahá,* flowering shrub so named

Bokṛo:ái, bokṛoi enái, bokṛọ kedeái, tickle

Bol á, } *boloi enái, bolo kedeái*,
Bolo: á, } enter, go in

Boláu:ái, boláu enái, kedeái, train (animals, &c.)

Bomál, to prove

Bombo, stupid, dull

Bon bonte,? net for fishing

Bond hoṛ, prisoner, convict

Bendo: á, bond enái, hedeái,[o] close (*e.g.* business, shop), shut up, end, finish

Bone badári,[o] highways and bye-ways

Bongá, demon, image, idol, ghost

Bongá soronjám, offerings

Bongá burái, *Bongái*, { perform rites, worship demons

Bo:ngái:, worshipper

Bongá rákáp, east

Bongá hásúro: west

Bor, *botor*, fear, danger

Bor ái, *Boro:ái*, } *boroi enái, boro kedeái*, fear, be terrified

Borkit,[o] blessing

Borlom,[o] spear, lance

Boro, the liver

Borod,, borod,,, very cleanly, tidy, neat

Boroi:, thin from disease, emaciated, withered; a kind of rice

Boron,[o] caste, complexion, colour, features

Boronj, perhaps, it might be, rather

Bostí,[o] village

Bosṭo:ái, bosṭoi enái, bosṭo kedeái,[o] be polluted, contaminated, defiled

Boṭkoi:, hill, mount

Botoro:ái, botor enái, kedeái, fear, dread, be afraid, alarmed;

Botoro:i:, coward

Botor o:choii:, an alarmist, frightener

Buang, kind of fiddle (made out of a pumpkin)

Bubrum, to hatch eggs

Buchạ: huchạ:, to snap off at the end

Buchái á, buchạ kedái, break off, snap off, nick off

Budá, shrubs

Buḍago: á, buḍạ: ená, kedái, break up (*e.g.*, the floor of a house), penetrate the earth (as a plough)

Buḍhá,† old man

Buḍhí erá, old woman

Buḍhá ápu ing, m, t, my, thy, his, grandfather

Buḍhí engá ing, m, t, my, thy, his, grandmother

Budh,† intelligence, knowledge

Budgárí, wisdom

Buglí, bag, purse

Buḍui: buḍujo: á, buḍui: ená, kedeái, bubble up; a disease in which the whole body is suddenly covered with spots

Bugi, good, nice, well, excellent

Bugi kathá, bugi juḍa, good news, Gospel

Bugi beohár, good conduct

Bugi assís, a blessing

Bugi sabiṭte, sahintte, } well (*ad.*)

Bugi ruaṛo:, to recover from sickness

Bugi bujháu, baṛái } like, approve of

Buhel, to flow, wash away

Buhídá:, wave, flowing water

Bujh,† understanding

Bujháu:ái, bujháu enái, kedeái, understand, discover, find out, comprehend, consider, conceive, experience

Bujháu ochoi, explain

Ing bujháure, in my opinion

Bujú bujú, innumerable, crowds (as ants), many

Buk áiái, ádeái, encourage, animate

Buhạ, navel

Buḷáu:ái, buláu enái, hedeái, seduce, deceive, tempt, mislead

Bulo:ái, bul enái, kedeái, be intoxicated, get drunk

Bulo:i:, drunkard

Bulú, thigh

Bulú jáng, thigh bone

Bulu chirit,,, groin

Bulu mayám, blood pricked from the body to expel evil spirits with

Bulung, salt

*Bumbui:,** a kind of fish [reflect

Bundis ái, kedeái, meditate,

Bunum, anthill

Bunum engá, queen ant

*Bunum baráṛe,** kind of wasp

Buráu: á, buráu ená, kedeái, waste, spend uselessly, injure, squander

*Buṛgí,** kind of giants who, in ancient days, killed everybody

Burú, mountain, hill

Buru burui ái, buru kedái, prepare land for sowing by breaking the clods

Burum ái, enái, kedeái, lie down (to receive a load as elephants or camels) sit on eggs, lie down in a den

Busạgái, busạ: enái, kedeái, hatch eggs

Busup, straw

Búṭ,† a kind of pea

Butạ, root

Butạre, under, at the foot

Butkí, yolk of egg

Buyut„ buyudo:ái, buyut„ enái, kedeái, throb, pain, tell anxiously

C

Chá:, wherefore? why?

Chabá: á, chabái ená, chabá kedái, accomplish, fulfil, end, complete, finish, abolish, dispatch

Chabá maráu:, die out

Chábug ái, chábu: kedái, take up in hand (liquids), put hand into (*e.g.* water to try if it is hot)

Chábuláu ái, kedeái, lick, suck

Chácharhát, rough and hard, crisp (as the skin after bathing)

Cháchási:, cultivator, husbandman

Chácho:ái, cháchoi enái, chácho kedai, toddle about, walk as a baby

*Chadi,** goat given by bridegroom to bride's friends

Cháḍo: á, cháḍoi enái, cháḍo kedeái, dip, bathe, throw upon the water

Chaḍor badoní, puppet, small wooden idol

Chaḍrá, bald

Cháechámpá, original country of the Sántáls

Chágáṛo: á, chágáṛ ená, kedái, split off or up

Chahábo: á, chaháp„ enái, kedeái, open the mouth, open (as a shell, flower, &c.)

Chaháu ái, kedái,° desire

Chahṭáu:ái, chahṭáu enái, approach, have access to

Cháicháite,? do something irregularly, or by guess

Chák, wheel

Chákdahaṛí, turban (like that worn by khidmatgars, &c.)

Cháko: á, chák ená, ádeái, aim at (with bow or gun)

Chákhái á, chákhá ená, kedái,° taste

Chakí, kneepan

Chakledár, kind of policeman

Chakmak,† flint

Chakṛá, eunuch

Chakrí,† service

Chál, frame of roof, roof

Chaláu: ái chaláu enái, kedeái, walk, move, go, strain off water, send, sieve, navigate (boat), distribute

Chalí,[o] custom, conduct, rites, tradition

Chál ái, kedái, hand from one to another, pass, give into hand

Chalan,[o] circulation, custom

Chámá chakar, a large bird

Chamár,† shoemaker

Chamḍulo: á, chamḍul enái, kedeái, splash in water

Chámkáu:ái, chámkáu enái, kedeái, to start (through fear, &c.)

Chamkạu:ái, chamhạu enái, kedeái, to whip, flog

Chámpá, a flowering tree

Chamṭá, leather rope for cart

Chámtáhí, woman with baby but no milk

Chámuk,† whip

Chánḍ, necessary, fated

Chándál,† wicked, villain

Chánḍo:ái, chánḍ enái, kedeái, press hard against

Chándo, God, the sun or moon, month

Chándo gáhaná:, the sun to be eclipsed

Chándo ráṇth, rays of the sun

Chándoro, licentious girl

Chánḍlom, chandbol, tail (of animals)

Cháng chungo: á, chung ená, kedái, finish to the last morsel, take away every scrap

Changá, side road, (*verb*) to branch off

Chánge,? fresh, active

Chánghe, ravenous, preying, (*metaphor*, oppressive)

Chánghe:, to lie in ambush, wait

Chápádo: á, chápát„ ená, kedeái, toss, cast, throw

Chapáṛo:ái, chapáṛ enái, kedeái, be possessed with demons

Chaple: á, chaple enái, kedeái, float

Chápo:ái, chápoi enái, chápo, kedeái, rest chin on hands, rest the hand (on something), handle, feel

Chapṛá, flat, level, even; cockroach

Chapúa, Sántál smith's bellows

Chárá,† fodder, food

Charak churuk, changeable, fickle

Chárchár, noise (made by scratching)

Charcháu: á, charcháu ená, kedái,° investigate, examine, spread, (as news)

Cháre: a straw

*Cháre kisní,** bird (so named)

*Chárit,,,** kind of grass

Chaṛháu: á, chaṛháu enái, kedeái,° come up, overcome (as sorrow, &c.) be angry

Cháṛháu, a play at Santal feasts

Chaṛíjo: á, chaṛí: enái, kedeái, hack off pieces, graze, just touch, chip off, break off

Chariodig,, around, all round, on all sides

Chárkhá, chárkhí, spinning wheel

Charnáu:ái, charnáú enái, kedeái, flog, whip

Charpoṭ, violence, oppression. tyranny, fraudulent, avaricious

Chás,° cultivation, agriculture *chás bás,* agriculture

Cháchási:, chás hoṛ, cultivator, farmer

Chás ái, kedái, cultivate

Chaṭíq, disciple, follower, pupil

Chaṭhí, slippers (leather below and rope above)

Cháṭo:ái, cháṭoi enái, cháṭo kedeái, swoon, be stunned with fear, start

Cháṭog ái, cháṭo: kedeái, lick

Chátom,° umbrella (of bamboo)

Chhottor, umbrella (of cotton)

Chátrá, having horns bent down (when one or both horns curve downwards)

Chhatrí,† a caste

Cháuká,? open place, extended field

Cháukathá, shelf

Cháukáu:ái, cháukáu enái, kedeái, be terror-stricken, be in consternation

Chaukidár,† watchman

Cháule,° husked rice (*cháṇwal*)

Chaunṛí,† plaited cowtails worn by women on the head, brush made of cow'stail to drive off flies

Chechlá, torch of split bamboo

Ched ái, chet,, kedeái,° learn, teach; mock, mimic, chaff

Chechet,, oṛá:, school

Cheti:, learned

Chepet,, ále, enále, advise each other, consult, mutually teach

Chedá:, why? wherefore?

Chedá: je, because

Chede:, bald on top of head

Chedir ái, kedái, have diarrhœa

Chedir bej,,, vomit and have diarrhœa, as in cholera

Chedro chedro, rough, uneven

Chehará,[o] nature, disposition, beauty

Chelá,† pupil, scholar

Chelá:ái, chelái enái, chelá kedeái, be or make disciple

Cheláng, pot

Chelko melko, wanton (woman,) forward, larky

Chele, who? what? what kind? which?

Chemeng, mongoose

Chenre, bird

Chenre chiprut,,, birds, fowl

Chepej ái chepe: kedái, suck, drink in

Cherchete:, lizard

Cherej ái, chere: kedeái, play with a child

Cheperej, talk with or amuse children

Chero bero: áko, bero enáko, kedáko, chatter (as birds or children)

Cherká bherká,? spotted, piebald

Chero, a coarse kind of grass used for rope (*juna*)

Chet, what? which?

Chetleká, how? as

Chet lagit,,, why? wherefore?

Chet chong, perhaps, who knows?

Chethon, something, a little

Chethon báng, nothing

Chet lekáná, what kind? what sort?

Chet tet,, *hon*, at all, in the slightest

Chetágo:ái, chetá: enái, kedeái, slap, beat, strike

Chetán, top, over

Chetánre, upon, on, over

Chetánte, upward

Chetán mohol, two-storied house

Chetánr, hardhearted, avaricious, miserly

Chetáu:ái, chetáu enái, kedeái,[o] regain (one's) senses, recover from drunkenness, become sensible

Cheter dhirí, thunderbolt

Cheter rŏte, tree-toad

Chhadáu: á, chhadáu enái, kedeái,[o] leave, omit, forsake, remit, escape, be delivered

Chhaḍwá, widower

Chhaḍwí, wife deserted by her husband

Chhai bolai, collection, all kinds

Chhailá chips, shavings, bark (of trees)

Chhálá, bullock or horse's saddle

Chhakáu: á, chhakáu kedái, strain of water

Chhále, cream

Chhallá badlá, bullock's load

Chhamḍá, a hut, (*i.e.* roof without sides for protection against the sun)

Chhánchhánáu: á, chhánáu enái, kedeái, smart, sting

Chhání: á, chhání ená, kedái,° strain (in a cloth), sieve, catch fish in baskets, &c.

Chhánkí jál,? small net

Chhapkáu:ái, chhapkáu enái, kedeái, crouch down, lie in wait

Chhapláu: á, chhapláu enái, kedeái, inundate, overrun, wash away, overflow, destroy

Chhápo: á, chháp ena, kedeái,° print, mark, stamp, seal, engrave, tattoo

Chhaprí,° hut

Chhaṛ, enclosure (for oxen), pen, fold

Chharrá chhiṭṭa,° shot (for gun)

Chhaṭiạr, baptism, naming the Sántál children on fifth or seventh day after birth

Chhaṭká, gate, door

Chhatná,? broad end of bamboo

Chhaṭpaṭiá, fickle, unsteady, fidgetty, troublesome

Chháu chháu, crowds on crowds

Chhaute,? vanish from sight

Chheilá, straight, erect, not stooping or bent

Chheo:ái, chheo enái, kedeái, bruise, slightly cut, graze

Chhero:ái, chher enái, kedeái, melt, dissolve

Chhilbiláu: áko, chhilbiláu enáko, ketkoái, jump, frisk about, leap, run about, bustle, be in trepidation

Chhilkáu: á, chhilkáu ená, kedeái, heave, spill as water

Chhín, appearance, form, shape

Chhinḍáu: á, chinḍáu ená, kettákoái, settle (dispute), arbitrate, unravel

Chhingáu: á, chhingáu enái, kedeái, stray, wander, separate from home friends or village

Chhirchhaturo: á, chhatur enáko, kethoái, scatter, disperse, turn topsy turvy, overturn

Chhitir bitiro: á, bitir enáko, kethoái,° scatter, disperse

Chhiṭkáu: á, chhiṭkáu ená, ádeái,° sprinkle

Chhiṭkiṉri:, switch, rod

Chhole: á, chhole enái, kedeái, rebound, glance off, fly off at an angle

Chhoṭ, time

Chhuchhi, reed

Chhuṉchhí,° nipple, teat, breast

Chhupí, umbrella-like hat of leaves

Chhurí,† knife

Chhuro:ái, chhur enái, kedeái, choke, suffocate in eating or drinking

Chhuṭáu: á, chhuṭáu enái, kedeái,° be dismissed, obtain leave; be clever, intelligent

Chhuṭkí, second wife

Chhuto: á, chhut enái, kedeái, defile, pollute

Chhut pheráu, repurify, perform ceremonies after childbirth or loss of caste

Chhuṭṭí, leave, permission, leisure, freedom, deliverance, dismissal

Chiạ: á, chiái enái, chiạ kedeái, frequent, investigate, examine, ascertain

Chiḍir, have the flux, menses, diarrhœa (see *cheḍir*)

Chigạri áiái, ádeái, mock, laugh at

Chigi:ái, chigi enái, fall on thorn or spike

Chiká: á, chikái enái, chiká kedeái, do, happen

Chiká chuno: á, chun enái, kedeái, break in pieces

Chikáṉr, clean, white, good (words)

Chikáṉro: á, chikáṉr enái, kedeái, polish, smooth, shine, be clean

Chiháte, how? why?

Chikijo: á chiki: enái, kedeái, slip on the back

Chiki: te, backwards

Chiknạ, sign

Chiknoṉ,† anise seed

Chilim,° pipe (for smoking)

Chin, chinhá, mark, sign

Chinháp, friend, guest, acquaintance, visitor

Chinpoṭ scoundrel, rascal, swindler

Chínṭ, paste ; to stick

Chínṭo: á, chínṭ enái, kedái, to colour, be spotted

Chintá,[o] thought

Chipạ, chirit., tight, narrow, small

Chír,[o] flag, sign, banner, end of turban left hanging

Chír ḍáng,[o] flag-staff

Chirái ái, enái, chirạ kedeái, tear, raven

Chirgálte, shyly, cautiously, timidly, suspiciously

Chiribiri, } spread out, torn in
Chiribiti, } pieces, rent in strips

Chirit , valley (see *chipạ*)

Chirit„ *hor*, narrow path, footpath

Chiṭáṉr, see *cheṭáṉr*

Chitiáu: á, chitiáu enáko, ketkoái, scatter, sow seeds

Chitháu, to sprinkle

Chitri, partridge

Chiṭṭá, shot

Chittar kabbar, spotted, variegated

Chiṭṭí, letter

Choágo: á, choá: enái, kedeái, nick off, break off, break in two

Choáṇṭiá, passionate, quick tempered

Chochongo:ái, chochongot„ enái, kedeái, sit on haunches

Chodogoi,* fish so called

Choḍor ái, kedái, make libation, offer drink-offerings, pour out a few drops before drinking

Choy ái, cho: ádeái, kiss

Chogoṛo: ái, chogoṛ enái, kedeái, be active, expeditious

Chohonko: á, chohonk enái, kedeái, dance, or walk, gracefully, adorn, ornament, dress neatly, arch the neck

Chohonk, ornament, adorning

Chohonṭ, rumour, news, tidings, noise of something, intelligence

Choilo, sharp, pointed ; a spike

Choká:, chohlá:, rind, peel, shell of egg ; proud

Choká: roṛ, speak irritatingly

Choká:gi, angrily, provokingly

Chokoj, to wash clothes

Cholono: á, cholon ená, kedái,[o] behave, act, conduct oneself

Cholon, currency, custom

Cholon idí, be the custom, prevail

Chondá pŏri, heap, pile

Chondái ái, ená, chondá kedái, heap up, pile up, put one on top of another

Chong, (in compos.) perhaps, (indefinite particle)

Chongá, pipe (made of bamboo, for distilling liquor)

Chonrhá: á, chonrkái ená, chonrká kedeái, seize person or property, put a mark on property, put straw upon a tree in jungle to shew it has been appropriated

Chopá kuṭạ, scoundrel, rascal, mischief, oppression, greedy

Chopíá, thin-faced, thin, light in the buttocks

Chopojo:ái, chopoi: enái, kedái, suck out, smoke (pipe)

Chopot chopot, noise as in kneading bread

Chopot,, chopot,,, low, low spot, cavity in the ground

Choṛáng, oblique

Choṛángo: á, choṛáng ená, kedái, fly off at an angle, glance off

Chorchoṭá, to provoke, speak in dispraise

Chorhod ái, chorhot,, kedái, kick, push with foot

Choro mokoi:, a kind of vegetable

Chorpoṭ, corrupt, treacherous, fraudulent

Chorṭhá, villain? impetuous, fiery tempered

Chorujo: á, chorui: kedái, put a few grains of rice on the ground before eating as an offering to *Bongá*

Choṭ, heaven, firmament, sky, air

Choṭo, mouse

Choṭokte, quickly, soon

Chuạ: á, chuại ená, chuạ kedeái, distil liquor

Chubạ:, something small in the eyes (*e.g.* dust, &c.)

Chuchu:, the female organ

Chuglá chuglí, chuglí, slander

Chuglí ái, ádeái, } slander, back-
Chuglí achur, } bite

Chugnui, to change from blossoms into fruit

Chúiṇ,? float of fishing line

Chuiṇhúr, sharp, pointed

Chuiṇyá:, scales of fish

Chukạ:, bottle, small earthen pot

Chuknrui, dish of leaves

Chulhạ, fireplace

Chumká: á, chumkái ená, be collected

Chumká áto, compact village (not like the long Sántál villages)

Chun,† lime

Chuno: á, chún ená, kedái, smear, plaister with lime

Chund, musk rat

Chunḍui:, wooden spoon

Chungur mungur, fickle, unsteady, coming and going, moving from side to side

Chupí, feather in bird's tail, tail of bird

Chupudo: á, chuput„ ená, kedái, give by handfuls, hold in fist, take a handful

Chuput„, handful

Chuṛa, crest of hill, pinnacle, summit, point

Churchuṭui:, said of children who do not grow either tall or fat

Chuṛin,* spirit or apparition of infant who dies before birth

Churú burú, brimful

Churui: cháule, rice put on ground as an offering to "Bongá"

Chuṭiá, a small kind of mouse

Chuṭuing muiṇ, black ant

D

Dá, potato, esculent root

Dá:, water, rain, climate

Dág ái, dá: kedái rain; string a bow

Dá: irchi, to sprinkle water

Dá: árej, bale out water

Dá: áting chenre, water wagtail

Dá: hásuro:, stop raining

Dá: loi, draw water

Dá: mándí, rice water

Dá: duḷí, midwife

Dá: tálá ghuṭú, island

Dá: tetáng, thirsty

Dá: sím, waterfowl

Dạd, a kind of itch on the hips

Dạn,[o] a witch

Dabáu eái, kedeái, threaten, forbid, pacify

Dabáu: á, dabáu enái, kedeái, overshadow, wear, cover

Dabí, agreement; shoulder-blade

Dabkáu: ái, dabkáu / *Dabṛáu: ái, dabṛáu* } *enái, kedeái*, crouch down

Dábo: á, dáp„ ená, kedái / *Dálobo: á, dálop„ ená, kedái*, } thatch, cover with leather

Dádá ing, m, t,,, my, thy, his elder brother

Ḍaḍḍí, well (in fields, not deep)

Ḍaḍḍu, large wooden paddle (to stir up the rice while it is drying)

Dádṇí,† advances (of money)

Dádrám, dárám, lead or conduct, support, come to meet (used only in compos.)

Dagá:ái, dagái enái, dagá kedeái, stop, hinder, cause to stumble, deceive

Dagá: dagág,,, jerk, twitch, entrap, ensnare

Ḍagḍagáu: á, ḍagḍagáu ená, flourish, be luxuriant (as trees)

Ḍagmagáu: á, ḍagmagáu enái, kedeái, rock, shake

Dágo: á, dág enái, kedeái,° mark

Ḍáhár, road, highway

Dahaṛí, turban

Ḍaháu: á, ḍaháu ená, kedeái, burn up

Dáhe, sour milk

Dahgí, household; family, race

Ḍáhi, manure heap, manured land

Ḍahi: á, ḍahi ená, hedái, blaze

Dahná, wages of a servant

*Dahu,** a kind of tree (so named)

Ḍahúro: á, ḍahúr ená, kedái, publish a fishing expedition

Dái, elder sister

ájing, elder sister

Daká, rice (boiled)

Dakái, to cook rice

Da: kái:, a cook

Ḍakáṛ ḍokoṛo:ái, ḍokoṛ enái, kedeái, bound up and down? jolt? walk as a very fat man does, waddle

Dakáu eái, kedeái, call on, invoke (demons)

Dákhílo: ái, dákhíl enái, kedeái,† make over charge, enter, deliver up, give in (rent, &c.)

Dáldáláu: á, dáldáláu ená, kedeái, shake, quiver

Ḍálí,† basket

Dalláhí, slough, mire

Dál eái, kedeái, strike, beat

Dál goi:, kill by beating

Dál petej,? snap at?

Dálob, see *dábo:*

Dámchá:, woolly haired

Dámdahe: á, dámdahe enái, hedeái, spread widely, be notorious, be renowned

Dámkom, calf, young ox

Dám ái kedeái,° make a bargain, price

Dán, gift

Dán ái, kedái, give

Dán águi, to bring, fetch

Dánángo: á, dánáng enái, kedeái, conceal, skulk

Dánáng peṛá, Satan, the devil

Ḍánḍá, loins, waist

Dánder, cave, hole of animal

Dándhái ái, dándhá kedeái, think, feel concern (see *dhandhá*)

Dándí, restlessness, care, sorrow

Ḍánḍitu, line (of book, &c.), handle (of umbrella, &c.)

Ḍánḍom, a fine, handle

Ḍánḍom eái, kedeái, to fine, punish by fining

Dáng, pole

Ḍang, heap

Ḍangauṛá, manure heap

Ḍángrá, ox, bull

Ḍángrí, cow

Ḍángrí oṛá:, cowhouse

Ḍangwá, unmarried, bachelor, virgin

Dáṇk, warmth, heat, flame

Dáṉrán ái, kedái, } walk about,
Dáṉrán baṛái, } wander

Dáṉre, dedicated, promised, an animal offered or dedicated to *Bongá*, sacrificial animal

Ḍánṭáu eái, kedeái,[o] improve, amend, rebuke

Dáṇṭ moṭ, strong (in legs and arms)

Dapá dapí, quarrelsome (woman)

Dápálo:ái, dápál enái, hedeái, hide, cover

Dápálo:, (mutual form of *dál*) beat mutually, fight, quarrel

Dáprám, (mutual form of *dárám*) meet by accident

Ḍaṛ, branch

Ḍaṛ ái, kedái,[o] run off, run away

Dárái kanái, approach, come near

Darái bongá, next month

Dárám, approach, come, walk (in compos.)

Dárám dá:, bridal ceremony, virgins take water and go out of the village to meet bride and bridegroom

Dáṛán ái, kedái, walk, go, travel

Dáṛán hoṛ, traveller

Dáṛáng, very steep, precipice, steep bank

Dáráng dáráng, very hot, blazing

Darbár ále, kedále, hold council

Darbár melá, court of justice

Daṛḍáhá, gormandizer, glutton

Dáre, tree, plant

Dáṛe, ability, power, strength

Dáṛe:ái, dáṛe enái, kedeái, be able, have force, prevail, overcome

Dáṛe habi:, up to one's strength, with all one's power

Dáṛe jokhe:, health and strength

Dáreáṇw,° sea, ocean

Dáreáfo: á, dáreáf ená, kedái,° investigate

Dáṛhá, dáṛhí, stream, river shut in by a band

Daṛiạ, obstinate, stupid, stubborn, thick, coarse

Dárí chhínál,° prostitute, courtesan, whore

Darkádále, having dishevelled hair

Darṛáu:ái, darṛáu enái, kedeái, slip, slide

Daṛú, powder, gunpowder

Daṛup ái, enái, kedeái, sit, rest

Daṛupá:, throne, seat

Dásáni, festival so called

Dasáu:ái, dasáu enái, kedeái, overthrow, knock down

Dastúr,† custom

Dátká oṛá:, kitchen

Ḍáṭom eái, kedeái, nip, pinch as lobster

Dátrom, sickle

Ḍáṭṭá, tooth

Ḍáṭṭá khorog,, set teeth on edge

Ḍáṭṭá uni, tooth brush

Dáu,° opportunity

Dáu:ái, dáu kedeái, obtain opportunity, win in a game

Dáuláu: á, dáuláu ená, kedái, cut up, mince, carve meat

Dáurá, a flat-bottomed basket

Dáwá,† to claim

Dawáṇw, to wander up and down

Dayá,† kindness, mercy, pity, favour, blessing

Dayáu áiái, dayá enái, kedai, be kind, shew pity or mercy

Dayá manáu, be kind, show pity or mercy

Dayá mayá, kindness

Dayági, piteously, helplessly,

Deá, the back

Deái ái, deá enái, kedeái, turn the back

Deáni:, security, one who goes bail

Dej ái, de: kedái, pluck flowers

De: chalá:, ride along, (mount and go)

Dejo:ái, de: enái, kedeái, mount, ascend, climb

Dekhense, give it!

Dekhitte,° knowingly, wittingly, with eyes open

Deko, the name given by the Sántáls to Hindoos

Delábo, come along (to many)

Deláng, come along (to one)

Ḍelem ḍelem, slowly, waddling along

Ḍenḍe,? bald, featherless

Ḍenḍká, featherless, tailless (bird)

Dene bánáren, umpire

Ḍengán ái, ḍengá enái, kedeái, wear, put on, dress (applied to men)

Ḍengáná:, garments, clothes

Deṛ, depeṛ, to copulate

Depeṛá johár, mutual salutation

Ḍerá:ái, ḍerái enái, ḍerá kedeái,† stay, stop, live

Dereng, diring, horn

Desápati,† ruler

Des mánjhi, the officer who oversees half of the Pargánas division

Dev, glory, majesty

Dev lekán, proud, glorious, haughty

Dháá,? weight put into scales to equalize them

Dhabáu, to put away (food, &c,)

Dháchri, mane (of horses, &c.)

Dhádráu ái, dhádrá ená, kedái, rend, tear, drag in pieces, be ragged

Dhádrá, full of holes

Dhákdhák botor, to be terrified

Ḍhaká ḍhakí, *Ḍhaká ḍhoko*, squabble, pushing and pulling

Ḍhaká bered, awaken by a push

Ḍhaká gnur, push down, cast down

Ḍhákái ái, ḍháká kedeái, push

Dhakuj, to squeeze, copulate

Ḍhál,† shield

Ḍhamkáu ái, enái, kedeái, upbraid, rebuke, succumb

Ḍhámpá ḍhompo, rough, uneven, unpolished, knotty (tree)

Dhandhái ái, enái, dhandhá kedeái, think of, be anxious for, be absorbed, feel concern

Dhandhá, employment
Dhandhá jong, be employed
Ḍhángo: á, ḍháng enái, kedeái, hinder, be obstructed
Dhandṛá dhundṛá:ái, dhundṛá enái, hedeái, bustle about, be in a fuss, make a hubbub, search about
Dhán rachág,? snap at
Dhánso:ái, dháns kedái, wander over, spread over
Dhapí, part of a fife
Dhárá, rule, rite
Dháráhí, steep, precipice
Dhaṛái ái, dhaṛá kedái, send forth a report, jolt against
Dhaṛás ái, enái, kedeái, let go, let fall (as spring, trap, &c.), discharge (gun)
Dharáu ái, kedái,[o] owe, borrow
Ḍharáu ái, kedái, smelt, cast, water at eyes
Dháṛdhuṛo: á, dhuṛ enái, kedái, search, make a noise in trampling
Dhari:, until
Dhársánr, slanting, inclined plane
Ḍhaṛwạ, branch (leaves and all)
Dhasáu: á, dhasáu ená, kedeái,[o] tumble in, slip into, sink, slip, give way
Dháu, time
Mi: dháu, &c, once, &c.
Dhedre, to become thin or worn out through age
Dhej, discreet; complete, perfect; fresh
Dhejo:ái, dhej enái, kedeái, spoil? complete, perfect
Ḍhekáro:ái, ḍhekár enái, belch, cough out
Dhelak,[o] clod of earth
Ḍhená, small
Ḍhenchogo:ái, ḍhencho: enái, kedeái, be lame
Ḍhenká,* "gendaliá" a kind of crane
Ḍheo,† wave, billow
Ḍher,† many, much
Ḍhero: á, ḍher ená, kedái, make addition, add much
Ḍher din reá, durable, permanent
Ḍher idi, continually increase, be on the increase
Ḍherá, hand spindle
Ḍhere ḍhere, intently
Dheyán, to fast (stay all night on the ground without eating, as Sántáls do before a "porob")

Dhidrik, bold, fearless

Ḍhikele, rich, wealthy

Ḍhiláu: á, ḍhiláu enái, kedeái,° despise, neglect, forsake, let alone, slight, let fall to ruins

Ḍhilí silí, laziness, idleness

Ḍhilwángo:ái, ḍhilwáng enái, kedeái, suspend or hang by hands

Ḍhimạli, idle, lazy

Dhináng, then, (future time)

Ḍhinki,° machine for cleaning rice

Dhinkíá, sportsman, archer

Dhiṉru:ái, dhiṉru enái, kedeái, be born, produce, spring, be pregnant, bring forth (young)

Ḍhíp,† island, coast, bank, shore

Dhípáu: á, dhípáu ená, kedái, heat iron, be eager, earnest

Dhiráu eái, kedeái, threaten, swear

Dhirí, stone

Dhirí chaṭání, rock

Dhirí káṭkom, lobster, prawn

Dhírijo:ái, dhírij enái, be pleased

Dhirjáu,? hush, be silent

Dhero:,? be patient

Dhirong sorongo: á, sorong enái, kedeái, become weak

Dhírpúro:ái, dhírpúr enái, kedeái, be satisfied, full

Ḍhitháṇw,° obstinate, sullen, sulky, bold, forward

Dhobí, washerman; a caste of cultivators

Dhobitásá, a low kind of grass

Dhodhoro, hollow, eaten away in the centre

Dhoká,† suspicion, suspense, doubt

Dhokdhokáu:ái, dhokdhok enái, kedeái, be in suspense, be in trepidation

Dhompo, wart in a tree

Dhon,° wealth, riches

Ḍhongá, boat

Dhopdhop ái, kedái, rap, knock at

Dhorá, dhorági, assuredly, certainly, doubtless

Dhoráu,° to hold fast, maintain, observe

Dhoro dhoro, unclean, untidy

Dhorom,° religion, righteousness, faithful, just, good, true

Dhoromo:ái, dhorom enái, kedeái, perform acts of religion, be true, or good

Dhorom pustak, the Bible

Ḍhuḍhuạ, small round pot, used for smelting metals

Dhukáu ái, kedái, blow bellows

Dhukdhukáu, to pant, be in trepidation (see *dhokdhokáu*)

Ḍhulá, a shelf, stand

Ḍhumbágo:ái, ḍhumbá: enái, kedeái, sleep or sit in a ball

Dhumdhárkánd, disorderly, untidy, unclean, out of repair

Ḍhunḍhá, ḍhunḍhí, foolish, awkward, dull: large bell hung on cows' necks

Ḍhunḍháu ái, kedeái, search, seek

Dhundhgí,° dimly

Dhuṉrá,° resin

Dhúp, two-edged sword

Dhúp jered, burn incense

Dhuṛáṇ dhúp, burnt-offerings

Dhuṛí,° dust

Dhurun,? to be dear

Dhurúp, flocks, shoals, herds, crowds; name of a tree

Dhusáu: á, dhusáu enái, kedeái, upbraid, rebuke, scold, find fault with, reject

Dhutí:ái, dhutí enái, kedeái,° dress, put on clothes (men)

Dhuṅáṇ,† smoke

Dhuṅáṇ rátá, soot

Diạṛá, candlestick

Dibí, image, idol

Díbo:ái, dib enái, kedái, swear, take oath

Díb ochoi, administer oath

Ḍig ḍig, bright (as fire), quick (as horse)

Ḍigáu: á, ḍigáu ená, kedái, be in vain, be useless

Digdháu:ái, digdhạ enái, kedeái, doubt, feel uncertainty

Digirdigiro: ái, digir enái, kedeái, beat dusty ground, come quickly, burn brightly

Digláu:ái, digláu enái, kedeái, prepare ground for seed? run off, raise the dust

Ḍih, village

Ḍih ghuṭú site of house or village

Dihiri, the person who performs "puja" before a hunt

Díjo:ái, dí: enái, kedeái, choke, strangle

Ḍiká ḍake: á, ḍiká dake enái, kedeái, shake about, from side to side, roll, waddle

Díl,† courage, bravery, courageous, brave

Díl áiái, enái, ádeái, encourage, hope, be brave

Díl báng dharáu, to despair

Dil dálo: á, dál ená, kedái, rock about, sway, jerk

Din,† a day

Din hilo:, *dingi*, daily

Dinám dinám, every day

Din kálom, last year

Din machhá, season, the the proper time

Din ṭaláu, spend time

Ḍinḍá, site of a house, home

Ḍingár, *ḍingrá*, impoverished, poor

Ḍing ḍabúr, to moisten, soak

Díní, part of crop given to repay reaper's work

Dípil ái, kedái, carry on the head, put on head

Diṛá mundte, firmly, earnestly

Diṛidáng, swollen (as a corpse)

Diring, *dereng*, horn

Disai ái, disa kedeái, remember, know, be aware, reflect, commend, praise

Disa ochoi, remind

Disom, country, kingdom

Ḍiṭom ái, kedeái, pinch (as a lobster), bite

Díuhe, candlestick, lamp, wick

Dob eái, kedeái, forgive, excuse, abolish, kill

Dobaṭia,° cross roads

Ḍobog ái, ḍobo: enái, kedeái, bow the head, stoop, bend

Dobṛá: á, dobṛá ená, kedeái, to double a string, clothes, &c,

Doboṛá,° double

Doboṛ, fold (twofold, threefold, &c.)

Dochŏt,, cock's comb (*metaph.* obstacle, *e.g.* an opponent would say, "I have a *dochot*,,")

Dodorosso, ill, melancholy, low-spirited

Dodosi:, accuser

Dŏg, a bud

Dog eái, do: kedeái, take by force, save, rescue, wrest off

Doh, go away! begone!

Dohái eái, kedái, appeal, arrest? attach,? pray, assist, help

Ḍoho, tumour, wen, wart in a tree

Dohoi ái, doho kedeái, obey, place, set down, put down, take care of, keep

Do: hoá,: a case (to put things in)

Doho gunjáu, keep back, withhold

Ḍoká, a kind of tree, "*jiá*"

Dol, a festival

Dol bahá, a flower used at the above

Dolá, palki

Dolán,° temple, big house

Domáu eái, kedeái, strike, beat

Dombo:, dumpling, cake made of rice

Dombol ḍombolo: á, ḍombol enái, kedeái, float

Ḍombráu:ái, ḍombráu enái, become thin, fade away; succumb, defeat, subdue; be silent from astonishment

Ḍomkáu: á, ḍomkáu enái, kedeái, spread, publish, be renowned

Dong, a game (at a wedding)

Donger, a game (at a hunt)

Dŏno: á, dŏn kedái, skip, to bound, leap, jump, spring, dance about, hop about

Ḍorá,† waist-string, girdle

Dorbár,° cause, suit, action at law

Doromo: á, dorom kedái, put, place, set down

Doro soro, unwell, indisposed, slightly ill, with a cold, low-spirited

Dos,† fault, sin

Doso:ái, dos enái, kedeái, be condemned, blame, accuse

Dosár hilo:, next day

Dosáu, to find fault, grumble

Doyog ái, doyo: enái, kedeái, be sick, loathe, vomit

Ḍuḍái, accusation, calumny

Ḍuḍurguju:ái, ḍuḍurgui: enái, kedeái, shiver with cold, tremble, coil up one self through cold

Dudurum, sleepy

Dudurumo:ái, dudurum enái, kedeái, nod (in sleep)

Ḍugí: á, ḍugí ená, kedái, prune a tree, cut the top of a shrub to make it thicker

Ḍugur ḍugur, to glare,? walk as a child

Duhará, again, once more

Duhará duhará, often

Duháu eái, kedeái, to milk

Duing duing bahá,* a kind of red flower

Dukh,† pain, affliction, distress

Dukhi, afflicted, distressed

Dukho:ái, dukh enái, kedeái, pain, suffer

Dukhí chárá, awkward, unfortunate

Dukh dukhwas, pain and trouble

Dulduláu: á, dulduláu ená, kedái, reverberate, thunder, roar, rumble

Dullạr,° love,

Dullạríyá, loved, dear

Dullạr eái, kedeái, love

Dulo: á, dul ená, kedái, pour (water, &c.) cast (metals, &c.)

Dul perej, fill up with liquid

Dumur, small bee

Dumur rasá, honey

Dundláu: á, dundláu enáko, ketkoái, spread, (as sponge, bread, &c.,) expand

Dundu, owl

Ḍunḍuk ái, kedái, to look about at night for something that has been lost, by the aid of a lighted stick, &c.

Ḍunḍukit,* a tree (so called)

Dún dún, piled up, (*e.g.* hair, &c.) loaded very high (as elephant, &c.)

Ḍungrí, hill, knoll

Dungut,, dungut,, hoṛ, crowds

Du̱nri, "*tudi*" eel

Dúrbín,† telescope

Ḍuriạ:ái, ḍuriạ enái, kedeái, adorn the hair with flowers

Duríb, a thing, article

Durum durum, crowded, multitudes (especially ants)

Duṛup ái, enái, kedeái, sit

Duṛup achur, sit in a circle

Durúso:ái, durús enái, kedeái,° arrange, adjust, scold

Dusáu,° blame, chide, be ashamed, (see *dhusáu*), find fault with (see also *dosáu*)

Dusku̱,° suffering, affliction, grief

Dusman,° enemy

Dwạr,° door

Dwạrí: hoṛ, doorkeeper

E

Ebheno:ái, ebhen enái, kedeái awake, be awake, arouse

Eḍhe:, to sit on one haunch

Eḍí,° heel

Edre:ái, edre enái / *Endre:ái*, } be angry, scold, murmur, be displeased, abuse

Edre, anger, malice

Edrete (*adv.*) against, opposed to

Edre sanging, to be angry with (*liter.* put one off in anger)

Eger ái, kedeái, abuse, scold, quarrel, (applied to women)

Epeger áling, enáling, quarrel mutually

Ehe:? alas

Ehe:? sob, wail

Eherte,? command, point out

Ehobo: á, ehop,, enái, kedeái, begin, commence

Ehob is 'to begin' from the present time

Etohob, 'to begin' in the past time

Eká jívi, desolate, lonely, entirely without relations

Ekáṛhá, alone

Ekkálte, all at once, straight on end

Eken, ekenạ́:, empty, hungry, idle, only, bare

Eken hoṛmo, naked

Ekená: lángtá, destitute

Eláng, splendour, glitter, glory, flame

Emán, emánten, emánteá, multitude, of all kinds, collection, assortment, appointment?

Emánem,? truant

Emo:ái, em kedái, give, bestow

Emo:i:, liberal

Em ḍengái, assist, pay another's debts (give and put on)

Em taláu, help

En betár, then, that time (past time)

En hilo:, then, that day (past time)

En párom, that side, over

En hoṇ, enkhán, then even, then indeed, still, *enkhánge,* then, that moment, (past)

En ḍekhán, then, in consequence

En ḍege, there, that place, yonder

En rehoṇ, en hoṇ, nevertheless, still

En drái, three days hence

En derese, then indeed (in anger)

Enáng, then, just now (past time)

Enḍágái, enḍá: enái, kedeái, mislead, set astray

Endre, scold (see *edre.*)

Ene:ái, kedái, dance, play, drill (as soldiers)

Engá, dam, mother, female, feminine

Engá jel, doe

Engá hopon or *hon,* mother and child

Engá káṭup, thumb, great toe

Engá payár, morning

Engáing, engám, engát,,, my mother, thy mother, his mother

Eno:ái, en kedái, thresh corn, tread out corn

Epelo: á, epel kedái, raise, lift up, (*i.e.* hand or stick to strike)

Epem, reciprocate, mutually exchange, mutually give, (see *em.*)

Epem chápáláu, assist mutually, give and take (from *em* and *chál*)

Eper áling, enáling, throw missiles, dust, &c., at each other, quarrel (from *er*)

Epṛe: áko, epṛe enáko, ketkoái, separate, divide, part asunder

Erá, wife

Erá hopon, wife and family

Erá miserá, sister

Eránḍom, castor-oil plant

Erbá, kind of rice

Eṛe, deceitful, false

Eṛe yeái, kedeái, defraud, inveigle, deceive, lead astray, cheat

Eṛeroṛ, to lie, speak falsely

Eṛe káthá, a lie

Eṛe idí, take away something under false pretences

Eṛgú, kind of red field mouse

Ero: á, er ená, kedái, sow seed

Esedo: á, eset,, enái, kedeái, surround, enclose, stop, hinder, shut

Eset,, achur, hem in

Esel, fair, white, light complexioned

Eser, be possessed, "jhapna" as *jogis*, seize, catch

Eshár, alone, lonely

Eshár re, in solitude, alone, privately, separately

Eṭá:, another, different, other, separate

Eṭá: ṭhen, in another place, in another's keeping

Eṭá: hilo:, at another time; reverse of fortune?

Eṭá: re, in another place

Eṭá: gárte, re-fashion,? change,? again, once more

Eṭá: hoṛ, } stranger
Eṭá: disomi }

Eṭá: muṭạn, eṭá: jŏntŏr, alike, resembling

Eṭá: mŏṇe, to think of something else, be absent minded

Eṭá: áimái joteko, commit adultery

Eṭá: bo: ngái:, heathen
Etáng, slight, thin
Eṭedo: á, eṭet" ená, hededái, enclose (with thorns), fence
Eṭet" achur, surround
Eṭet" achurá:, fortifications fence
Ethem ái, kedái, attract attention by coughing, hem
*Etká,** a kind of creeper
Eto, nevertheless
Eto:ái, etoi enái, eto kedeái, instruct (a beginner) train (men or animals) [time), (see *ehop"*)
Etohop", beginning (in the past
Etom, right hand
Etomo:ái, etom enái, kedeái, baulk, be on the right hand
Ewero: á, ewer enái, kedeái, to fan, blow

F

Fasal,† harvest
Fakat,† only
Fhaḍ, army
Fharák,° different
Fharáko: á, fharák enái, kedeái,° separate, go apart, be different
Fhasád ochoi,° to slander, backbite, calumniate
Fhiriád ái, ádeái,° sue at law

G

Gábáu ái, ená, kedái, two sowings of rice, to dye
Gábe, marrow
Gáblái yái, gablá ená, kedái, tie in a bundle
Gachháu:ái, gachháu enái, kedeái, receive, admit, confess
Gachhí, sprout, young plant
Gachhí: á, gachhí ená, shoot (as a tree), become big enough to transplant (as rice)
Gaḍ, concourse, crowd
Gádá, heap, pile
Gádá gud, confused heap or pile, confused noise
Gáḍá, river, stream
Gaḍái yái, gaḍá ená, kedái, excavate
Gádár, unripe, not yet dried, (*e.g.* grain)
Gaḍáu: á, gaḍáu ená,° operate (as medicine), influence, bury in, impress, fix
Gaḍbaḍáu: á, gaḍbaḍáu ená, ketkoái,° blunder, confuse
Gaḍḍí† throne
Gadel, herd, flock, multitude
Gadhá,* donkey, ass

Gáḍhá goḍhá, rough, coarse work, uneven, unfinished, very big

Gaḍí,[o] cart, carriage

Gaḍí áto, dense village

Gaḍí:ái, gaḍíenái, kedeái, inhabit, dwell, (particularly animals)

Gádlá:, excavation, pool, deep pit

Gadṛá, coarse, thick (as water when dirty)

Gadur ái, enái, kedeái, scratch with nails

Gádut, bold, forward

Gáo,† cow

Gáe káṛá (káḍá), flocks, cattle

Gáe pál, herds of cows

Gáe chúr, a place where there are many paths

Gág ái, gá: kedái, weave, spin (as a spider or man)

Gahánr guhunr ái, kedái, talk gently, whisper

Gahí, decoy, decoy bird

Gai gám eái, ená, hedeái, tickle, gently feel, slightly rub

Gaing guingno:ái, guing enái, kedái, mutter, talk in a low voice

Gáigájáu: á, gajáu ená, be heaped together so as to rot, to heat

Gájár, dense, thick jingle

Gájáro:, to be in difficulty

Gákhur, well acquainted, informed, accustomed, clever

Gáláe, small grass, quantities of fish

Gálám gálám, indistinct

Gáláng ái, kedái, braid, weave, plait

Gáli, button-hole, loop, loophole

Galát,, *soládo:*, to faint? be foolish ?

Galáu: á, galáu ená, kedái,[o] fuse (metals), slacken (lime) smelt, melt, adjust (differences)

Galáu legát,, *ái*, *legá: kedái*, test metals

Gálmaráu ái, kedái, converse, discourse, argue, debate, explain, consult upon

Gálmaráu, conversation

Gám, story, fable

Gám gum ái, enái, lurk about, skulk about

Gámpátáu:ái, gámpátáu enái, be sullen, sulky (as one when awaked from sleep)

Gán, about, nearly

Gán, to copulate

Gánári, small fishing net (round)

Ganbúr, a big piece of wood with a hole in it to let the water through

Gandár gundur, muttering

Gánde ái, kedái, cross, lay one on top of another, interrupt, put something to stop the way

Gandhak,† brimstone

Gandhit, "karait" a small poisonous snake

Gánḍ garuṛ, rhinoceros

Gánḍo, small wooden stool

Gangít,† stones from which lime is made

Gání sání, mislaid, uncertainty, forgetfulness

Ganján, to crush under foot

Ganjiạ, purse, bag for money

Gáno: á, gán ená, kedái, concern, be right, satisfy, agree, suffice, hold out, be sufficient

Gáno: khán, if, perhaps

Gáno: dhari:, until then, until it shall be enough

Gáṉrá,* "kachu"

Gáṉrke block of wood

Gánṭ,† joint of tree, knot

Gápá, to-morrow

Gáfilo:ái, gáfil enái, kedeái,° loiter, be careless

Gaṛ, difficulty, trouble, danger

Gáráng dá:, water from a sore, matter

Gárdí, clubman

Gárgádlá, abundant, ample

Gárgári,* white flower, growing amidst rice

Gargaráu:ái, gargaráu enái, kedái, gargle, take water into the mouth and eject it on a person as witches do, to oppress

Gaṛh,† fort, castle

Gaṛháu ai, kedái,° make, fashion, form, conceive in the womb

Gaṛí, monkey

Garí: á, garí enái, kedeái, brush along before, sweep along before

Garjáu ái, kedái, mourn, wail, weep, cry, roar, growl

Gaṛmág ái, gaṛmá: enái, kedái, be slow of speech, stammer

Gároi: sároi:,? filthy

Gársílom, dim, indistinct, unclean, badsighted

Garúr, "*gharúr*," adjutant bird

Gasá gasí:ái, gasí endi, come in contact, rub against

Gásgás ái, kedái, scratch with nails

Gási, to fart, make wind

Gáske, strainer

Gásmanḍáu: á, gásmanḍáu kedái, tread up (as cattle would a road)

Gáte, friend, acquaintance, companion; with, in company of

Gáte:ái, gáte endi, kedeái, to accompany, associate,

Gáte gáte, together

Gáṭhiá, stumpy, sturdy

Gawíj,, ái, gawi: kedeái, beckon (to come)

Gawi: goḍá eái, kedái, wink at

Gáyá, capon

Gáyám gáyám, crawling sensation over the body

Ged ai, get,, endi, kedeái, cut, sever, pare, scrape

Get,, páṛág, split in two, halve, cleave

Geḍe, duck (tame)

Gedrá, Satan

Gej ái, ge: kedái, clean rice with hand from the vessel in which it was cooked, stir up in a pot, scrape

Gejer ái, ená, kedái, break in pieces

Gejerá:, rice broken to pieces, any thing broken up, pieces, crumbs

Gele, ears (of dhan, &c.)

Gele: á, gele ená, shoot (as dhan)

Gelej ái, gele: kedái, dig and carry off, excavate

Gemeṛ ái, kedái, carry, bear a load

Gendṛá, torn garment, old piece of cloth, rags, bits of clothes

Genḍwar, sling

Gene: gene,? go in flocks, go in herds, shoals

Gengáhi, crooked

Genthe, to copulate as dogs

Ger ái, kedeái, bite

Geper, bite mutually

Geráng ái, kedái, gasp, groan (in sickness)

Gháne gháne, again and again, repeatedly, continually

Ghangero:ái, ghanger endi, turn aside from a road

Ghángŏrá, a bean

Ghánṭí,† small bell

Gháo,† a rub, sore

Ghaṛ, ambush, a pass, strait

Ghardí jawágni, one who pays for his wife by working in his father-in-law's house

Ghardwárá,† family

Ghaṛí,† hour, clock

Ghárontji,° master and family

Gharṛí, ladder

Gharwá, sparrow

Ghás,† grass

Ghásí, grasscutter

Ghasáu ái, kedeái, cleanse, scour, scrub

Ghásráu ái, enái, kedeái, drag along the ground, haul along

Gháṭ,† ford, landing-place

Gháṭ dár, toll-keeper

Ghaṭáu: á, ghaṭáu enái, kedái,° diminish, lessen

Ghaṭáu gnindá, just before dawn

Ghaṭí ái, kedái,° commit a fault, endure loss, be blameable

Ghaṭí ená, it was too little

Ghaṭí, sin, crime, fault, sinful

Ghátí, clever, cunning

Ghaunsí eái, kedeái, to take along with, associate with, take into company or union, &c.

Gheṇṭ,† pack, bundle

Gheṇṭ ái, kedái, pack, wrap up, tie up

Gheorá, whirlpool, eddy

Gherá, (a kind of) tambourine

Gheráu eái, kedeái,° surround

Ghiri áiái, ghiriạ kedeái, revolve, whirl round

Ghŏnghŏr, hollow trees

Ghoṉrá eái, kedeái, carry a child astride on shoulder

Ghoráu: á, ghoráu ená, kedái, mix, dissolve

Ghoráu mid,,, mix together

Ghoṛí, time (see *ghaṛí*)

Ghoṛí ghoṛítigi, in an instant, every moment, immediately, quickly

Ghor korná, stores, chattels, effects, property

Ghulghuláu:ái, ghulghuláu enái, kedeái, be restless from heat, be very warm, heat (as hay, &c.)

Ghunghurú, bells (for the ancles)

Ghuṉrá, string of a bow

Ghunṭí,° knee

Ghusáu:ái, ghusáu enái, avoid meeting, shun

Ghuṭu, elevated land, the high land (on which villages are built)

Gidi,° eagle, vulture

Giḍi ái, kedái,° cast away, throw, put down

Giḍiá:, rejected

Giḍí sái, throw away, reject

Gidirá, child, infant, childhood

Gidirá pidirá, children

Gidirá jong, to have a family

Gijiri: á gijiri ená, be curdled, become sour (as milk)

Girá, intelligence, news (particularly of a marriage or death), knot

Giri, to cut into logs

Girjá,† church, Christian worship

Giṭa, string of tongue

Giti:ái, gití enái, sleep, lie down

Giti: i:, sleeper

Giti: daṛup lie with, sleep with (a wife)

Giti: báṛái, go to sleep

Giti: jiráu:, rest by sleep

Giti: oṛá:, bed room, dormitory

Gitíl, sand

Gitíl ái, kedái, scour, wash, scrub (chiefly vessels)

Gnám ái, ená, kedeái, find, obtain, want, seek, receive, acquire, demand, get

Gnágnámi:, seeker

Gnám baṛái ái, kedeái, wander in search, look about for

Gnám ruaṛ, regain, recover

Gnám gnúm, to get by asking

Gnánwán ái, search for, want

Gnápám áling, en áling, mutually want, marry against friend's wish, meet, join } mutual form of *gnám*

Gnápámo: á, gnápám ená, be fulfilled, accomplished, happen, come to pass } mutual form of *gnám*

Gnápám gnupum, twilight

Gned eái, gnet,, kedeái, assault, hit, colour, dye, stain, bewitch

Gneped, assault mutually, contend, fight

Gnepe: i:, assailant

Gnet,, goi:, kill

Gnel ái, ená, kedeái, see, look

Gnelo: á, gnel ená, appear
Gnelo: habi:, visible, as far as eye can reach
Gnel me, behold, lo
Gnel hor } wait, expect
Gnel dárám }
Gnel hayám, a glimpse
Gnepel, have an interview, meet
Gnel ṭhík, } recognise
Gnel oporom, }
gnel orom, }
Gnel orom, knowledge
Gnepel oporomko, acquaintances
Gnel gelá:, to try, test
Gnel ochoi, show
Gnel sahí, correct
Gnel baṛái, search for, look about for
Gnel saṇwhái, investigate

Gnele, bee
Gnele rasá, honey

Gnindá, night
Gnindá bhŏr, all night
Gnindá chándo, moon
Mi: gnindá, } all night
Goṭá gnindá, }

Gnindír, white ant

Gnir ái, enái, kedái, escape, fly, flee, run away
Gnir bŏl kedái, elope, (a girl going to a man's house)
Gnir baṛái, jump about, run about
Gnir haparáu, race
Gnir chalá: } run off
Gnir seno· }

Gnong, a little (in compos)

Gnonhod eái, gnonhot„ kedeái, to brush slightly against

Gnúi ái, gnu kedái, to drink
Gnúgnúá: ? a cup
Gnúgnúi: a drunkard
Gnúṇyá, a drink, potion, cup
Gnubhuchaṛ, very drunken person, habitually drunk
Gnuṇgnui: a wet-nurse, suckling
Gnu áikáu taste

Gnukor, tremulous (referring to the head or body)

Gnúmo: see *gnutumo:*

Gnuṇrá, hiccup

Gnuṇrui:, * "*sanári*" a tree

Gnuro:á, gnur enái, kedeái, fall, throw down, descend

Gnutum, name
Gnutumte, by name, concerning
Gnutumo: } *ái,* &c., be
Gnumo: }

named, famous, be well reported of, be disgraced

Gnutum dohoi, to name (a child &c.)

Gnutum ákán, renowned, famed

Gnum en, named, called

Gnupum, to exchange names

Bahaná gnutum, the name given to a person afterwards (to distinguish him &c.) [name

Mul gnutum, own original

Gobolo:ái, gobol ená, kedeái, have authority, have power over, be in power of

Gochhá yái, kedái, tie, carry in the bosom

Gochhá, cluster, bundle, something wrapped up in corner of the *chaddar*

Gocho, moustache, beard; *mangrí gocho*, moustache; *sakwá gocho*, whiskers

God ái, got,, kedái, pluck, pick fruit flowers, &c,

Goḍ lagáu, salute

Goḍa, high ground fit for crops other than rice, garden (at some distance from the house)

Godor, stout, fat, fat-faced

Goḍhe eái, kedeái, fondle, play with (as a child and his mother)

Godhro, fat, lazy, thick, (as muddy water)

Goḍo, rat

Godor, stout, fat

Gog ái, go: ádeái, promise, confess, agree, admit, take on shoulder, undertake, acknowledge

Gogoing, gogom, gogot, my, thy, his, uncle (father's elder brother)

Gohá,° witness

Gohá gujráu, bear witness, bear testimony

Gohanáu eái, kedeái, search for prey, hunt after

Gohodom, stubborn, obstinate

Gohŏṛ ái, kedeái, trail, drag

Gohún,° wheat

Goi: hoṛ, corpse

Goju: ái, goi: enái, kedeái, die, expire, kill, slay

Goj eái, goi: kedeái kill

Goi: baṛíjo: to die

Gol mirich,† pepper

Gol muṛía,° round (perfectly round, as a ball)

Gomket, master of a family

Gondráu:ái, *gondráu enái*, *kedái*, growl

Gong eái, *kedeái*, give a girl in marriage, answer to a call, respond

Gongrod,,o:ái, *gongrot,, enái* be hoarse (from cold &c.)

Gono: custom

Gonom, the marriage portion

Gŏnŏng, price, money given for a girl at marriage,

Goṉre, saddle for bullocks &c. panniers, large bundle, name of tree

Goṛ, cowhouse, stable

Goṛi:, *guṛí:*, cowdung

Goṛij ái, *goṛi: ená*, *kedái*, smear, plaster with cowdung

Goráso:ái, *gorás enái*, *kedeái*, be civil, polite, seek after, keep, support, receive into house

Gorás sáṇwháṇ, receive friendlily, take care of, be kind to

Goṛet, bailiff who helps to collect rent

Gorlá, spotted, piebald,

Goṛo, to help, assist

Goro: goro: heartily

Gorob hoṛmo,° pregnant

Gŏrŏj,° necessity, occasion, desire

Gorojo:ái, *goroj enái*, *kedeái*, love, like

Goroming, namesake

Gosejo:ái, *gose: enái*, *kedeái*, clean the head of vermin

Goso:á, *gosoi ená*, *goso kedeái*, wither, fade

Goṭ, herd, flock

Goṭá, all, entire

Goṭá ṭánḍí, every place

Goṭá leg, complete, finish off

Gotáu ái, *kedái*, fit on (one thing on another), be gathered, confess, adjust, put sword in sheath

Gŏtŏm, ghí

Gotor kathá? sluggish

Gŏtoro: á, *gŏtor ená*, *kedái*, run (as fire in a jungle) spread

Gŏyŏn ái, *ená*, *kedái*, break down standing rice

Guá, betel nut

Guchháu:ái, *guchháu enái*, *kedeái*, destroy, kill

Guchhí, bundle

Guḍguḍáu:ái, *guḍguḍáu kedái*, toss about, (as water) roar, thunder

Guḍṛá dwarf, short

Gudrí, goat-house, sheepfold

Guḍur guḍuro: to be nimble, to trip lightly

Gugui ái, enái, gugu kedeái, carry on, or suspend from, the shoulder behind

Guguri, a small bird

Guher ái, ádeái, shout to, call aloud to

Gulánḍ, round (but long, as a round stick)

Gulánj, a kind of tree with flower white and yellow in centre

Gulí,[o] ball, pill

Gulíbánṭo: ále, gulíbánṭ kedále, cast lots

Gultí? gossip, prate, tattle

Gúm ái, kedái, winnow

Gumá ? mouldy, dusty

Gumánte, according to

Gumo:? fade away, dry (as leaves)

Gunḍí, cow used to the plough

Guṇdráu:ái, gundráu kedái, growl

Gungú, hood made of plantain leaves

Gungudo: áko, gungut,, enáko, ketkoái, to gather under wings (as a hen does)

Gunhá,[o] sin, wickedness

Guni bhábi:ái, bhábi enái, be thoughtful, anxious, solicitous

Gunjráu:ái, gunjráu enái, kedái, growl, roar, cry out

Gunsí, silver &c. chain worn round the waist

Guntí:ái, guntí enái, kedeái,[o] esteem, look upon, deem

Gupí, cowherd

Gupí ái, kedeái, tend cattle

Guṛ, treacle

Guṛákul, tobacco (prepared for smoking)

Gurguṛáu: á, gurguṛáu ená, kedái, gurgle (as a hukka)

Gurguráu: á, gurguráu ená, kedeái, whirl round

Guríb, guni guríb,[o] poor, abject, needy

Gurláu: á, gurláu ená, whirl round (as smoke)

Guro:ái, gur enái, kedeái, fall

Gurú,† charmer, conjuror, teacher, fortune-teller

Guṛúmo: ái, guṛúm enái, be silent, remain quiet, cower

Guṛúm dohoi, delay, put off

Gusáu: á, gusáu enái, kedái, break (covenant, &c.) cross over

Gusti, generation

Guṭek, many, numerous

Gutí, slave, servant man

Gutiyá, tribe, relatives (connections who will eat, but not worship, together)

Gutui ái, ená, gutu kedái, string beads, flowers, &c., weave, stick on, fix on

Gutului eái, enái, gutulu kedeái, tickle

Gyán,† knowledge

H

Hábág ái, kedái, aim at (with arrow)

Habbuk ḍabbuk dá:, wave

Habbuk dabbuk eái, kedeái, threaten

Habi:, until

Haburu:, to eat any thing by jerking into the mouth with open hand

Hadáb, to take and eat some and throw away the remainder (*e.g.*, eat the grains and throw away the stalk)

Háḍáp,,, to nibble, munch, eat as mice do

Haḍgár, a kind of wolf

Hádhád, rushing, impetuous (chiefly of water)

Haḍi:ái, haḍi enái, kedeái, dislocate neck, put in stocks

Hados, to be sorrowful, be sad

Háemoikát enái, kedeái, startle

Hahaṇkár, barren, sterile, wilderness

Háháṛá, miracle

Háháṛá:ái, háháṛá enái, kedeái, be amazed, astonished, wonder, admire

Háhás, affliction

Hahí dudí, oppression

Háhut, glutton

Hai, woe!

Hai haio:ái, haihai enái, kedái, *Hai soe*, } mourn, groan, sob, wail

Hairá gairá, to be confounded

Hájám ái, kedái,† cheat a creditor, digest

Hájot,† prison, confinement for a few days

Háko, fish

Háko íl, fins

Hakráu:ái, hakráu enái, bellow (as a bull), pant

Háláng ái, kedeái, choose, gather, select, pick up

Halái halái hoe, a storm

Háláí ái, hálá kedái, ransom, pay, atone

Háládwáráu,? ransom by paying another's debts

Halbal, mischievous, naughty, wanderer, vagabond, commotion, excitement [flower

Hal bahá,* a kind of white

Háledále, be astonished, perplexed, in difficulty, in doubt, be homeless, friendless, vagabond

Hálim,* a tree so called

Hálo bálo, halbalíá, restless

Haloi, pounce as a hawk

Hamá hŏmo, to threaten, rebuke, take by force

Hámál,† heavy, pregnant

Hámálá:, a burden

Hámrám, polished, elegant, clean, tidy

Háṇ, heṇ, yes

Háná, hánáṭá, that, the furthest, the first named

Háná purí, the future world

Háná sá / *Háná se:* } that side

Hánái:, that person, the furthest one

Hándere / *Hántere*, } there (far off)

Hánáte, thither (far off)

Háná:, "mirghi," a kind of fit

Háná: goju:ái, goi: enái, to have fits

Hánḍá, large earthen jar

Hánḍí, the intoxicating liquor made from rice

Hanhár, mother-in-law, wife's mother

Haṇo:ái, haṇ enái, kedeái, condemn, prove guilty

Há̱nrá hápe:ái, hápe enái, kedeái; be silent as midnight

Há̱nrobo: á, há̱nrop,, enái, kedeái, catch hold of, catch in a spring

Há̱nru, large monkey

Háṇs, háṇsíl, two birds, male and female, from which, according to the Sántál mythology, all living creatures sprung

Haṇsí uḍáu,° sneer, scorn, ridicule

Haṇsu, haso, pain

Haso edingná, kedingná, pain, hurt

Hanur jhanur,? tinkling

Hápám mundo: / *Hápám bundo:*, } to sleep together

Hápámun, grown up girl, a girl who has reached maturity

Hápcháporí,? clapping of hands

Hápe:ái, hápe enái, kedeái, be silent, cease, hush, wait

Hápe thiro:, be patient, have patience

Hápe hápete, quietly, secretly, privately

Hápen, futurity, future (in compos.)

Háp̣ṛá:, great, big

Hápṛámko, the ancients

Haptáu áling, enáling, debate, dispute

*Hápuko:,** a kind of small bird

Hạr ái, kedái, collect, sweep up with the hand, deliver to prison

Hará:ái, harái enái, hará kedeái, grow up, increase, become big

Hará en } adolescent, grown up, adult, arrived at manhood
Hará en buru en }

Háṛám, old, old age

Háṛám buḍḍhí, husband and wife

Háṛám jokhái, old age

Haráṉrá, gills of a fish

Harbá, a small animal so called

Harchát,, hurchot,,, rough, uneven

Hárdund, rebellious, self-willed, violent, obstinate

Háre pháre, quickly

Haṛhát,,, bitter

Háṛhát,, sisir, gall

Haṛí, put in stocks, fetter, see *haḍí*

Haṛí biṛí, prisoner

Haṛiá gaṛiá, confounded

Hariạṛ, greens, herbs; blue, green

Hariạro:, to blossom

Haṛing, father-in-law, wife's father

Hárká, a covered basket

Hárkedo:ái, hárket,, enái, kedeái, trouble, be grieved, pained

Hárket,,, trouble, annoyance, grief, pain

Hárono:ái, háron enái, be perplexed, be in trouble

Háṛsuṛo: á, háṛsuṛ ená, get low, (fire, candles, &c.), cease, stop

Háṛtá, skin, leather, hide

Hartáu áiái, hártá ádeái, serve food

Háṛubo:ái, háṛup,, enái, kedeái, embrace, seize

Hápáṛub, mutually embrace

Hárub ái, hárup" kedeái, cover up, confine, turn over

Háṛum táṛum, in haste

Has, pretty, desirable

Haso:ái, has ená, ádái, desire, long for

Hásá, earth, soil, ground, land

Hásá leká, brown

Hasái khilái,° mirth and sport, play and fun

Háso, pain, (see *háṉsu*)

Háso háron, pain and suffering

Hásúro:ái, hásúr enái, set (as sun or moon), clear off after rain

Háṭ,† market, fair

Hátá, fan (for winnowing grain)

Hatá badi áling, enáling, vie, contend

Hátáng, brains

Hatáu ái, kedeái, take

Hathauṛi, hammer

Háth chuṭṭí,? active

Háthí,† elephant

Háthí sunḍá, ivory

Háthlá:, armpit

Hathyar,° weapons

Háti,? importune

Háting yái, ená, kedeái, share, distribute, divide

Háto,* aunt, father's sister

Háturáu ái, kedeái, grope in the dark

Háubháu, friendship, mildness, gentleness

Háuháu ái, kedái, make a noise

Haunḍí, exacting, exorbitant, violent, oppression

Háuráu, to abuse

Hauwá dukh,° cholera

Házíro:ái, házír enái, kedeái,† attend, be present

Heḍejo: á, heḍe: ená, kedái, boil, bubble up

Heju:ái, he: enái, come

Heju: seno:, come and go, pass by

He: kedái, he plucked

Helá, timber, wood

Helá sáhán, wood for [burning

Helá helí baṛái, be a vagabond, wander about

Helej" ái, hele: kedái, cut, slash

Heṇ, yes

Heng ái, kedái, receive, admit, agree, acknowledge, say yes

Heṇ huiṇ, agree together, consent mutually

Hená, probably

Heṇchong, perhaps, it may be

Hende, black

Hendeá:, blackness

Hendero: á, hender ená, kedeái, grow dim (*e.g.* eyes by working at night)

Hendo:? sit or be idle

Hendrá, featherless, with uneven wings

Henglá, poor, hungry, dirty

Henk henkte, violently (particularly of weeping)

Henrem, sweet

Henremá: sweetness

Heo eái, enái, kedeái, carry on hip, nourish, nurse, bring up children, take in bosom, support

Heo jong, have children

Heo hárub, nestle, cling to one's mother

He:oi:, heheoi:, a nurse

Hepetáu? to envy

Hero:ái, her ená, kedái, trim a tree, wear away by use (*e.g.* knife, pencil)

Here, chaff, husks

Herel, hepel, man

Herel leká, manfully

Herhed ái, herhet" kedái, weed a garden

Herhenjáng, straight tree without low branches (*e.g.* palm)

Hermedo:ái, hermet" enái, kedeái, carry under arm

Hesá, "pipal" tree, ficus Indicus

Hese:ái, kedái, prune a tree, lop off, cut off branches

Hesel, "dha," a tree

He: setero:, arrive (see *heju:*)

Hesráu ái, enái, kedeái, pant, be out of breath, be parched

Hetáu ái, kedái, observe, obey

Hetet" ái, provoke, irritate (apparently there are no past tenses)

Hetet" gi, obstinately

Hewá:ái, hewái enái, hewá kedeái, to form habits, be accustomed to

Hewel, hewer, bitter

Hichchha,° wish

Hichkáu:ái, hickkáu ená, kedeái, be in perplexity, feel disgust

Hiláu:ái, hiláu ená, kedeái,° move

Hili, sister-in-law (eldest brother's wife)

Hing hanu ái, kedái, neigh

Hinostá eái, ená, kedeái, to contemn, despise

Hinrihi, tall and slender (like a palm)

Hipir,* a kind of tree

Hiqqe:,⁰ right, due

Hiráng petáng, sick man's gait or conduct; dirty vessel

Hiri eái, kedeái, visit, go to see

Hipiri, visit mutually

Hiri agui, visit

Hirij ái, hirí: ená, kedái, spill, fall about, be scattered

Hiri: pasíro:, fall in all directions

Hiṛing nái, kedái, forget, be careless

Hirkáu áiái, hirkạ ená, kedeái, hate, be disgusted with, despise

Hirkạ pirkạ, contempt

Hirká:ái, hirkái enái, hirká kedeái, trust to, hope in

Hisạb,⁰ accounts, arithmetic

Hisạb kitạb, bills and accounts

Hisạb ái, kedái, keep accounts, calculate

Hiskáu áiái, hiskạ ádeái, be proud, boast, envy

Hipiskạ, to vie, contend mutually, feel rivalry, quarrel

Hiskạ holong, pride, conceit, arrogance, envy

Hissaliá, slander, backbiting

Hissi, a kind of small bird

Hitáu: á, hitáu enái, kedeái, be accustomed to (see *hetáu*)

Hiyạting, darling

Hiyạtingno:ái, hiyạting enái, mourn for

Ho, hoihoi, yes, that's true, quite right

Hoboro:ái, hobor enái, kedeái, lie or hold in lap

Hod ái, hot„ kedái, pluck ears of corn, pull out the grains by running the hand up

Hodo:, quickly (in compos)

Hŏe, wind, climate

Hŏe ŏṭángo: á, oṭáng ená, kedái, blow up by the wind

Hŏe dá:, storm

Hŏe bajáu, the sound of the wind

Hŏe eddái, ledái, blow

Hoho: áiái, ádeái, call

Ho: hoi:, crier

Hoho sor,⁰ call to one

Hoi hoi, quite right

Hoi daṛe, be possible

Hoing háring,* father in law (wife's father)

Hokko pokko, quickly

Holá, yesterday

Holát,,, razor

Hŏle? if then, perhaps, probably

Hŏle khán? perhaps (uncertainly)

Hŏlŏng, flour, meal

Hŏlej ái, hŏle: kedái, pluck ears of corn, nip off

Hol kálom, three years ago

Holong, flour, meal

Homoṛ, to weep, mourn, be sad, be absorbed in

Homoro: ái, homor enái, kedeái, be soft, humble, gentle, meek, lowly

Hoṇ, even (in compos)

Honáng, perhaps, probably

Hoṇ choṭo, mouse

Honḍág, to stir up while boiling

Honjángo:ái, honjáng enái, kedeái, tumble over or into, slip into, roll over or into

Hopoho, call mutually (see *hoho*)

Hŏpŏn, child, son, young, small

Hŏpŏno:i:, pregnant

Hŏpon erá, daughter

Hoputet,,, dispute

Hor, road, path

Hor udui, to guide, show the road

Hor agui, to make a road

Hortenko, passers by, travellers on road

Hoṛ, a man, a Sántál

Hoṛ goi:, murder

Hoṛ, marry a girl to a man

Hoṛet, pod

Horhoi ái, horho kedái, watch, guard, defend, protect

Horko jánge, fence in, keep within an enclosure, guard carefully

Hoṛmo, the body

Hoṛmo berelo:, bear children

Hoṛmo: ái, hoṛmoi enái, be pregnant

Hoṛo, huṛú, paddy, rice in fields

Hŏrŏ, tortoise

Hoṛo hoṛo, man by man, one by one

Horog,, *ái, horo: kedeái*, wear (clothes)

Hosor giḍí, have a miscarriage

Hoṭág ái, hoṭá: kedái, stir up, rip

Hoṭá: orej, tear in pieces, rend (with teeth)

Hoṭo:, neck, throat

Hoṭo: tolá:, neck tie

Hoṭor ái, kedeái, probe a wound, lift up, scrape off, rub away, take out

Hottete, on account of, by means of

Hoyo:ái, hoyoi enái, hoyo kedeái, shave, peel

Hoyu: ái, hoi enái, kedái, be, suffice, become

Hoyu: ot, fertile ground

Hubág ái, hubá: kedái, chop, split, cut up

Huchạg ái, huchạ: enái, kedái, break off (*e.g.* a branch from tree), break (heart, &c.)

Hudạ,[o] office

Hudạí eái, enái, hudạ kedeái, send from village to village (the Sántál way of forwarding things)

Huḍing, little, small

Huḍing tárásing, about five o'clock p.m.

Huḍing dá: lo ber, about six p.m.

Hudís ái, kedái, plan, invent, think

Hudís ochoi, remind

Huḍu huḍui:, a little, some

Huduṛ huduṛ ái, kedái, thunder

Hugui: hoe, light wind

Huhár, pigeon

Huḍhuḍáu: á, huḍáu ená, kedái, murmur (as water) rumble, rustle, thunder, roar

Hujúrre,[o] apparently

Hukái, to snort as a bull

Húk,, húk,,, bitterly, violently (as a person weeping)

Hukum,† order

Hukut,, hukut,, dying? at the last gasp? bitterly (crying)

Húlo: úle, húl enále, kedále,[o] excite mutiny, rebellion

Huhuli:, a rebel

Hulár? sling

Hulsing ái, kedái, sharpen (iron) resharpen, put edge on

Hunar,† art

Hundạṛ, wolf

Hundṛáu, to growl, roar

Hupkạ, suddenly, at once (any unbroken event, *e.g.* a storm, a peal of thunder)

Hupṭi:, low (people,) humble, inferiors, poor

Huṛá huṛí, busybody, pushing person, a pushing and pulling, rapid, ceaselessly

Hurkạṉr,[o] bolt of door, to bolt

Huṛu, rice in field (see *hoṛo*)

Huṛu huṛui:, some, a little (see *huḍu huḍui:*)

Huṛung ái, kedái, husk (rice)

Huṛung bhugạg, break or make a hole (see *bhugạg*)

Hurut„, stump, root (of tree &c. left in the ground)

Husíd ái,. *enái, kedái*, pare

Husnạk ái, kedái, ornament, adorn

Huṭhuṭú, lofty, high

Hutum, to wash mouth

Hutí, a small insect bred in rice

Huṭí, to become weak

I

I:, dung, excrement, rust in iron, refuse of iron, lead, &c.

Ijo: á, i: ená, kedái,

I: jŏng, go to stool

I: kunḍ, hell

I: oḍok, refine metals, &c.

Íạ, means, device

Iạte, by means of, on account of

Ibíl, thick, dense (as foliage, *dhán*, &c.)

Ichạ: prawn, shrimp

Ichá: bahá, a kind of wild flower

Idi ái, kedeái, to take away, conduct, lead

Idi águi, to bring back, restore

Idi torái, carry off, take away

Idi harái, carry off some person

Iḍí,⁰ ancle, heel (see also *eḍi*)

Ijárá landlord

Ijárdár, agent, rent collector

Ikakái ái, ikạ kadái, leave off, let go

Ikṛumo:ái, ikṛum enái, kedeái, kneel, bend the knee

Íl, quill, feather

Ílo: á, íl ená, kedái, become winged, to feather (arrow, &c.)

Ilák chhaḍá,⁰ separate from, leave, part

Ímboro, boro, the liver

Íná:, ínábaṛe, ínáge, thus much or many, so much, as much as

Ínáte, ínáterảng, *Íná mente*, therefore, for this reason

Íná lehá, like this

Indárá kúiṇ, zigzag steps to a well

Ingodo: ái, ingot„ *enái, kedeái*, bend, stoop

Ingongte,? enigmatically, obscurely

Iṉrijo: á, iṉri: ená, kedái, extinguish

Ipil, star

Ír:ái, kedái, reap

Íro: jokke:, harvest time

Irchí ái, kedeái, ádeái, sprinkle, spatter

Isí, twenty ; plough beam

Isín ái, ená, kedái,° cook, boil, melt away

Isiṛ ái, kedái, grin, smile

Ishir, to rub

Istahár ái, kedái,° advertise, publish

Íta, seed

Íṭá,° brick

Itaṭ,,, remnant, leavings

Ithulát,? always absent from home

Itíj, to pinch

Ítíl, lard, grease, fat

Itkido: ái, itki: enái, rub the eyes

Itud eái, kedeái, paint a girl's forehead (at marriage)

J

Jáage, as much as?

Jábráhí, handsome, beautiful, middle-height, middle-sized (man or animal)

Jáegá,° place

Jáe koráṛ,* great grandson

Jágír,° land free of rent

Jáguár eái, kedeái,° watch

Jáháṇe, whoever

Jáháṇ, jáháṇná, jáháṇge, whatever

Jáháṇte, jáháṇre, anywhere, wherever

Jáháṇná: te, in any way

Jáháṇ kaháṇ, here and there

Jáháṇ leká, like which, how

Jáháṇ lekáte rehoṇ, somehow or other

Jáháṇ tíná:, as much as

Jáháṇtís, whenever, what time

Jáháṇ hilo:, whenever, what day

Jáher thán, sacred grove near each village

Jáher erá, the goddess who lives in the above

Jáhere? to court (a woman)

Jáhíro: á, jáhír ená, kedeái,° show, publish, expose, make clear, make known

Jáijug, eternal

Jaijulm,° oppression

Jájánámi:° producer, creator

Jájánámkin,° parents

Jál ái, enái, kedeái, lick with mouth

Jaládo: á, jalát„ ená, kedeái, stick, cleave to, adhere

Jálaní:, fisherman

Jalá púrí, the ocean, sea

Jalí, blossom

Jálo, a kite, (a bird)

Jámbe, jaw, jawbone

*Jámboṛo,** large snake "dhomna"

Jámin,† bail, security

Jamíndár,† landlord

Jámká, tree thick enough to make two ploughs

Jamkí, girdle, chain, round the waist

Ján, ján gurú, prophet, wise man, magician, sorcerer, revealer of secrets

Jánámo: ái, jánám enái, kedeái,° arise, be born, be produced, breed

Jánám hilo:, birth-day

Já: ánámí:, creator

Jánám bhŏr, } all life
Jánám jug, } long

Jáng, bone

Jángá, leg, foot

Jángá latáro:, be submissive, subject, be obedient

Jánge, rails, fence, slight hedge

*Jánhe,** wild grass, "khodo"

Jani:, about, nearly, perhaps

Jánko: ái, jánk kedái, be earnest, hearty, strict

Jánkte, heartily, strictly, with all the heart or power, necessarily

Jáṉrí, hemp

Jáṉri kichri:, coarse clothes

Jánte, mill stones

*Jánte,** pumpkin

Jánúm, thorn

*Jánúm bele,** "bair", a thorny tree, fruit bearing

Jánwár,° animal

Jápágo:ái, jápá: enái, kedeái, rest on something, lean for support

Jápíd ái, jápít„ kedái, close (the eyes)

Jáput„ rainy season

Jápud ái, jáput„ kedái, rain

Jaṛáu:ái, jaṛáu enái, be sick, be ill

Jaṛhí,° fountain, spring

Jaṛi ái, kedái,† fall (as rain)

Jáṛí,? ulcer

Jaṛmaṛ, weeds

Jarndi, insects (bred in rice)

Jarŏng jarŏng, scarlet, very red

Ját,† caste

Jatá:ái, jatá enái, kedeái, become dirty

Játá, sticky, gummy

Jáṭá, hair done up in a knot, lock of hair, tuft

Játur, skip about (as a bird), hop about

Jáu hilo:, continually

Jáuge, every day, always

Jáurá: ále, jáurái enále, jáurá ketkoái, assemble, collect

Jáwágno: ái, jáwágn enái, kedeái, marry, couple, take a husband

Jáwágni:, married (man), husband

Jáwátenkin, twins

Je, jemŏn, that, so that, in order that

Jedero:ái, jeder enái, kedeái, warm oneself in sun

Jel, meat, deer

Jelo:, be refreshed after weariness, grow warm after cold, recover, pull up

Jeleng, long, to lengthen, extend

Jembed ái, jembet„ enái, kedeái, drink by putting down the mouth, suck

Jenjle, beg, importune (as beggars)

Jenkete,? virginity

Jered„ ái, jeret„ enái, kedeái, burn, light, fire off gun

Jereṛ ái, ená, kedái, clean (the floor) smear with earth smoothly

Jerke:, copulate (as dogs)

Jeṭh hopon, eldest son

Jhabráu, bind round, wrap round

Jhaiṇyo:ái, jhaiṇ enái, kedeái, faint, be insensible

Jhak jhaká:, brightness, splendour

Jhál, warm (as pepper)

Jhál edingná, it burns me

Jhálí, jál, net, snare

Jál uḍáu, trap, snare, ensnare, spread net

Jhaljhaláu:ái, jhaljhaláu ená, kedeái, glow, glisten, shine as sun or moon

Jháp jhápá, very sleepy, nodding in sleep

Jhalkáu: á, jhalkáu ená, kedái, burnish, varnish, polish

Jháne japáne, flowery, bearing flowers luxuriantly

Jhangá, trousers, pantaloons

Jhanjhanáu: á, jhanáu ená, dry (as grain in sun) be crisp (literally, to tinkle)

Jhanjhát, very dry, dried up

Jhánh, a lever

Jhanká jhakuro: á, jhakur ená, kedái, be tangled, be in great confusion, be broken in pieces

Jhánkár, a buck

Jhankaráu, to complete

Jhánṭí,† fence, hedge

Jhanur jhunur, tinkling

Jhaṇṛráu: á, jhaṇṛráu ená, kedái, wither away

Jháṛá, a kind of wild useless rice

Jharáu: á, jharáu ená, kedái, repair house, run as a sore

Jhaṛáu ái, kedái, notch, pare, scrape

Jháre eái, kedeái, extract poison by rubbing, use charms or incantations

Jháṛ jhuṛ, crashing noise

Jháṛ jhuṛo: á, jhuṛ ená, kedái, wave (as corn) shed (as grain)

Jharkáu: á, jharkáu ená, kedái, burn

Jharpá, splendid (used of trees)

Jháṭá, frame for vines

Jhaṭás ái, ená, kedeái, beat against (as wind) strike upon

Jhíj ái, jhi: ená, kedái, open (door, box, &c.)

Jhili, fireplace

Jhilo:ái, jhiloi ená, jhilo kedái, hang suspended, swing

Jhimbiri, net made of bamboos

Jhín, jhín báber, bridle

Jhinjhináu:ái, jhinjhináu enái, kedeái, faint (with hunger, &c.)

Jhink, porcupine

Jhink ái, kedái, strengthen by tying, support by tying, lay in order

Jhonḍ, dense jungle

Jhonk mariá, of own accord, of itself

Jhorá koái, ketkoái, drive along, brush along

Jhuláu:ái, jhuláu enái, kedeái, be very ill and weak

Jhumká, bells for ancles

Jhunḍ, bush, (also *jhonḍ*)

Jhunko:ái, jhunk enái, kedái, be brave, mighty, courageous, active, energetic

Jhunk em, fight well or bravely

Jhunur jhunur, tinkling

Jhur á, ená, kedái, choke up, overshadow

Jhuṭh pus,° false, pretending, simulating

Jhutiáu eái, kedeái, catch hold of

Ji ái, kedái, smell, snuff

Jibí, jiwí, soul, spirit, constitution

Jiwí jaṭí, all kinds of creatures, living things

Jiwet,,, life, alive, living

Jiwí ráṛej, kathá, consolation, comfort, encouragement

Jiwí judaṣi ái, enái, kedeái, be comforted, consoled

Jiwí anmanáu, amuse

Jiwedo:, to live

Jiwet,, dá:, cold water, running water,

Jiwet,, háṛtá, living creatures

Jiwet,, moto, jiwet,, habi:, all life long, until death

Jiwí lo, to be sorrowful

Jiwí agui, take the life of another

Jiwí gnur, be disappointed, disheartened

Jiwí dhirí, a certain white stone

Jigirte, importunately

Jíhú,* a kind of small bird

Jiki:, to walk on all fours

Jíl, deer, meat, flesh (see also *jel*)

Jilpudo:ái, jilput,, enái, sit helplessly

Jináu:ái, jináu enái, kedeái,° escape, be victorious

Jir,* a kind of gum

Jiráu, rest

Jiráu: ái, jiráu enái, kedeái, to rest

Jiráu: maháṇ, sabbath

Jirá,† a spicy seed "jírá"

Jirit,, jirido: á, jirit,, akáná, glisten, shine

Jirmogo:ái, jirmo: enái, kedeái, be disfigured, appear sad, look dejected, be weak from hunger

Jiṭa bhor,° all life long

Jitáu:ái, jitáu enái, kedeái,° conquer, overcome, win

Jiwán,° young

Jo, jos, fruit

Jo:á, jo ená, kedái, bear fruit, be united

Jo bahá din, fruit time, harvest time

Jo bahá:, to flourish, bear fruit, be prosperous

Jobáb ái, kedái,° answer for, account for

Jobḍháu, to wallow, roll in

Jobṛá, chips, parings, filth, atom, mote, dust, shavings

Jodo: ái, jo: kedái, obliterate, rub out, wipe

Jog,[o] worthy

Jog ái, jo: kedái, sweep, wipe, clean

Jojo: i:, sweeper

Jo: gáṛi:, preserver, advocate

Jogáṛte, carefully

Jogáṛo: ái, jogáṛ enái, kedeái, *Jogáu*, } keep safe, take good care of, provide for, watch

Jog mánjhi, the person who arranges the marriages of the young

Joh, circumstance

Johá, cheek

Johár ái, ádeái, make obeisance, salute, bow

Joi ái, en tingná, aim well, hit mark

Joj, great

Jojáu ái, kedái, spend (life &c.), live, keep alive

Jojo, acid, sour, tamarind, sorrowful

Jojo rasá, *Jojo kanji*, } vinegar

Jojo ? haughty, proud

Jo: joháu, standing ready, prepared

Jojom, right hand

Jojon, a distance of about thirty-two miles

Joká, a worm (in cattle)

Jokár ? young

Jokhá, occasion, time, opportunity

Jokhái ái, jokhá kedeái, compare, match, measure, adjust accounts

Jŏkŏnŏdo: ái, jŏkŏnot,, enái, become hungry, wither, get old (as a woman)

Jŏkhŏn,[o] when, at what time

Jolá, marsh, lake, "jhíl"

Jolo:ái, joloi enái, jol kedeái, blaze or burn, set fire, light, scold, be angry

Jolo: ángrá, jolo: koilá, burning coals

Joloá:, splendour

Jol rákáp, blaze up

Jolom ái, kedái, plaster coarsely

Jom ái, kedeái, eat, consume, suffer

Jom god,, to finish eating

Jŏmŏk, crowded

Jŏmŏk áko, enáko, hetkoái, *Jomkáu*, } dance and play ? (as a crowd), collect in numbers

Jomot ? agree

Jŏndṛá,[o] maize, "jánerá"
Jŏne, wart (on body)
Jonk,† leech
Jono, broom
Jŏnŏ, servant
J·páting, greens, vegetables
Jor ái, enái, kedái,† fight bravely or well, use force, coerce
Jorwár,[o] strong, strength
Jor bajor,[o] forcibly, violently
Joráu: ái, joráu ená, kedeái,[o] couple, pair, fasten together, yoke
Joṛháto:ái, joṛhát enái, kedái,[o] join hands, salute, beseech
Joṛí,[o] mate, pair
Joro: á, joroi enái, joro kedái, drop (as water in drops), leak, ooze out, shed (as tears)
Jŏrŏ: ái, jŏrŏ enái, kedeái, warm self
Joṛo, part, share, divide
Jos ái, kedeái, aim at, level bow or gun, hit mark
Josáu: á, josáu enái, kedeái, injure, hurt, lose
Jot,† the whole of one's land
Jote, a yoke, the rope on a bull's neck
Joṭed,, ái, joṭet,, ená, kedeái, touch
Joṭij ái, joṭi: enái, kedái, give more, give again, add
Jot,, jot,, ái, ená, kedeái, rub (with oil, water, &c.)
Jŏto, all
joto pakháre, all round, on every shelf
Joton eái, kedeái, keep safely, guard, preserve, protect, help, take good care of
Jotonte, carefully, safely
Jowáu:, fit, proper, useful, suitable
Juáb áiái, ádeái,[o] answer, dismiss
Judạ eái, ená, kedeái,† separate
Judi,[o] if
Jug,† ages, perpetual, continual
Jug sengel, perpetual fire
Jug chŏlŏn, old customs, traditions
Juhaṛáu: á, juhaṛáu ená, kedái, get ready, collect together
Julut,, juludo: ái, julut,, ená, kedeái, be drowsy, slumber, nod, glimmer, appear (as a little fire)
Jumáu: á, jumáu ená, ketkoái, accompany, collect, get ready
Jungi: ái, jungi ádeái, be addicted to, be zealous, be fond of, earnest for

Jupi, a class of Brahmins who sell beads, &c.

Juṛáu ái, ená, kedái, collect, get ready, prepare

Juṛí,† companion, comrade, couple, pair, compare, suit, apply

Juṛí jotá: } marry
Juṛí pari: }

Jut, good, ready, repaired

Jut aikáu, like

Jut ámái, ádeái, kedeái, be kind, repair, mend, improve

Jutaráu: á, jutaráu ená, kedái, mend, put in order, repair

Juṭáu: á, juṭáu ená, ketkoái,[o] give, obtain, get, find

Júti,† shoes

Juṭij, see *joṭij*

Juwán,† young

Juwáu: á, juwáu enái, kedái, strengthen

K

Kabá: kabágo:ái, kabá: enái, kedeái, gallop (as horse)

Kabá: kobogo: á, kobo: ená, kedái, hit against, strike against (as a plough on a stone)

Kabrá,[o] piebald

Kachá kuchạ: á, kuchái ená, kuchạ kedeái, squash, bruise into a jelly

Kachahrí,† court of justice

Kachní, petticoat, skirt of clothes, part of *dhoti* which hangs in front

Kachṛáu eái, enái, kedeái, dash down, stumble, fall on face

Kachráu ái, kedái, cut off (American whitling)

Káḍá koḍo eái, kedeái, stoop, be lame in walking (through an injury to foot), limp

Kaḍí, pumpkin; young buffalo (female)

Kádráu eái, kedeái; *ái, kanái, ádeái*, be angry, incensed, indignant

Káenḍe, unripe

Káerá, plantain

Kafhariáu:ái, kafhariáu enái, dispute, quarrel

Kágáṭ,[o] paper

Kaháni,† fable

Káhilo:, be emaciated, attacked by illness

Kahiṉsáu eái, kedeái, be annoyed, disturbed, vexed, angry

Káhú,† crow, raven

Kahubutte,* a kind of tree

Kạí ái, kedái, sin, commit fault

Kailá, hour

Kaingchur, skin of snake

Kaingchur lekáná, fine (as clothes, &c.)

Kaipí, an ugly girl

Káj,† labour, work, business

Kajiánw, caution, circumspection

Káhá ing, káhám, kákát, uncle (father's younger brother), my, thy, his

Káhante, about, concerning

Káháti, wife of father's younger brother

Kákṛá, lizard of a large species [woman

Kálá, kálí, deaf man, deaf

Kálhuṛí, young who have left the dam

Kalí,† ink

Kálkáláu eái, kedeái, make a noise, make a row, create disturbance

Kálom, next year

Kálŏṭ, young hen

Kámár, blacksmith

Kám bhánḍori,[0] awkward, lazy, one who spoils work through inattention

Kámbŏrá,[0] blanket

Kámdá, to copulate

Kámí,[0] business, labour, work, action

Kámí eái, kedeái, work, employ labourers

Kamnrí, servant woman

Kánárí, arrow head

Kánḍá, earthen pot, "ghaṛá"

Kándet,, kándedo: ái, kándet,, enái, kedeái, become weak, roll about (as a sick or drunken man)

Kandhá, room

Kándi, pit of *ḍhenki*, in which rice is pounded

Kandor, place of fear, place of terror (*e.g.* some dark spot in the jungle)

Káno kánoto, repeatedly

Kánghár, deadly?, fatal?

Kangkhá, rim or mouth of vessel

Kánrá, kánrí, blind man, blind woman

Kánrá ghákŏr,* large fish

Kánrbá, plough handle

Kánrbiárá:,* a kind of fruit or vegetable

Kánrchu, iron spoon

Kanrí eái, enái, kedeái, commit (to prison, &c.), deliver over (see also *khanri*)

Káṇt, earth wall

Káṇṭá, throat

Kanthá, quilt, pieces of cloth put under a baby

Kanṭhár, jack fruit "kaṭhal"

Kaṇwárite, earnestly, heartily, diligently

Kápál,† forehead, fate

Kapchí, scissors, cut with scissors

Kápelgáe, wild cow

Kaphariáu, quarrel (with words) be contentious (see *hafhariáu*)

Kápí, battle-axe

Kápu,* a kind of potato

Káṛá, *káṛí*, buffalo (male and female)

Karáhí, large pot which becomes gradually wider towards the top

Kárám,* a kind of tree, "kaim"

Káṛáng káṛáng, dense, dark, thick, murky

Kárár,† covenant, agreement, arrangement

Kárár kathá, agreement

Kárbár ái, *kedái*,† trade

Kaṛchung, tall, thin, lanky

Káṛe, refuse of plant from which oil has been expressed

Káṛgo, attack, oppress, be violent

Karhạí ái, *karhá enả*, *kedái*, level land after ploughing, harrow (an instrument drawn by oxen and chiefly used in drawing earth to make "bánds")

Karháṛ, two bars at entrance of enclosure,

Karígol,° workmanship

Karíndáng, dense, thick, black (as clouds)

Kárlá,* a kind of fruit or vegetable

Kárnete, on account of

Karsáṉr,* a reedy grass

Kasá, unripe, stringent

Kasáu ái, *hedái*,° load, fill (pipe, gun, &c.)

Kási eái, *enái*, *kedeái*,° castrate (see *khassi*) a wether

Kasi, *kasigele*,* coarse, reedy grass, with white flowers like pampas

Káskom, cotton

Kásmár,* a kind of tree

Kásoi ái, *enả*, *kedái*, make folds in cloth, plait

Kásrá, itch

Kastáu: ái, *kastáu enái*, *kedeái*, apologize, express grief, repent

Kátá, saw

Káṭá, leg

Kaṭh,† wood, timber

Kathá, a word, order, saying, speech

Kathá oṛe eái, kedeái, persuade

Kathá kátáu ái, kedái, disprove

Kathá baḍái, knowledge, eloquence

Kathá dá:páli, conniving at a fault, concealing a crime

Kathá phạnḍáui:, one who contradicts both parties

Kathá seṭer, give or receive notice

Katháe, namely, that is to say, viz.

Kaṭhináu:ái, kaṭhináu enái, kedeái, be numbed

Katí, a play, round pieces like draughtsmen

Káṭí:, small, very small

Káṭí: táláng, very small, a little, in the slightest

Káṭi: chulung, very little (in degree)

Káṭ jibá,[0] be a deadly enemy, feel deadly enmity, be cruel

Káṭhom, lobster

Káto, knife (of *dom*)

Kaṭrá kuṭrá,[0] pieces, chips, break in pieces

Káṭup, finger, toe

Káṭup udug,,, rebel

Káucháuṇ eái, enái, kedeái, be disconcerted, scream, be angry

Kaulau:ái, kaulau enái, kedeái, be disturbed, disquieted

Kaumau:ái, kaumau kedái, make a noise

Kauṛi,† small shell (used for coins)

Kawar awar, noise, row

Káwe:,* a small red seed "rati"

Káyán, sour, cross, crabbed, quick-tempered

Kazák,,, strong, earnest, firm

Kechág ái, kechá: ená, kedeái, divide eatables, break bread, break up to pieces

Keched,? to hit by accident

Kechel ái, ená, kedái, separate the broken from the good rice with a fan

Kecho bedṛo, chirping of birds

Kedár, mark on a woman's forehead

Kedo: dáká, supper

Keing meing, be quarrelsome, contentious, chattering

Keklesedo:ái, kekleset,, *enái, kedeái*, be confounded, be in terror

Kelhát,,, broken pieces, chips (of pottery &c.)

Kenderpe:, ugly girl

Kendri bánám, a kind of musical instrument made of a pumpkin

Kenryot,,, scream of cock

Keontá,° boatman, fisherman

Kere, a furnace

Kere: mete: eái, hedeái, be in pain (as a woman) hold with difficulty

Kerker, a stiff neck

Kerkero:ái, enái, hedeái, strut about? swell with pride, have a stiff neck

Kete:, stiff, hard, firm, covetous, hardhearted, cruel

Ketel eái, enái, hedeái, feel sudden fright, startle, start

Ket ketej eái, kete: enái, hedeái be insensible (as a dying person), be stiff and cold

Kewá, chin

Khaas, ringworm

Khabar,† tidings, news, intelligence

Khabelá, very large field

Kháchár, resolute, determined, firm

Khachla:, basket

Khád, leafless

Khád,° manure

Khádú, stem of tobacco plant

Khadbadáu:ái, khadbadáu enái, hedái, be in suspense, in trepidation, in distress, stick in mud

Khádle eái, enái, kedeái, throw into, cast into

Khadro khodro, jagged

Khagáu: á, khagáu enái, kedái, decrease, diminish, become less

Khái khabro:, lament, regret, be sorry for something

Khái khoi ái, enái, whisper, be dumb

Khaiyu:, pit

Khajarí,° rice parched, "*morhá*"

Khájná,° rent, tax

Khájná tahsíl ora:, collectory, where rents are collected

Khájná uthátu, collect rent

Khálai, grass basket

Khallá, plate of leaves

Khám khuntí,† post, pillar

Khámború, religious teacher, teacher of charms

Khamcháu eái, enái, hedeái, snap at, bite, seize by the claws

Khámdá eái, enái, hedeái, gambol, sport, a kind of play

Khámsáu eái, kedeái, gallop
Khán, if (in comp.)
Khaṇaṣ, ringworm? a kind of itch on the side
Khánchá, cage
Khánḍá, stick used in sword dance, weapons
Khándá, brother in law, (wife's brother)
Khanḍá hunḍí ái, hunḍí kedeái, bruise, beat into pieces
Khándá purús, the height of a man with hand raised up
Khandaṛáng, gulf, abyss
Khanḍí, woman's *sárhí*
Khándlá: khondlo:, rough, uneven
Khándo khápuá, toothless
Khándrí, deep, to deepen
Khangoṭ, dried up, burnt, parched, (as a desert)
Khanjáu ái, kedái, weigh in mind, calculate, ascertain, establish
Khánjo eái, enái, kedeái, let down, fall down, slip into
Khánri, cave, cavern, depth, difficulty (see *kánri*)
Kháp, steps to mount by, notches
Kháp kháp, correct, true, truth
Kháp̣rá,† tiles
Khaṛ, herd of cattle, flock
Kháráq ái, khárá: kedái, spit, have phlegm
Kháráhí, earthen pot, (see also *karáhí*)
Kharái, threshing floor
Khaṛá: kanái, khaṛá enái, kedeái,† be ready, be at hand
Kháráng khácháng, ill nature, cross, bad tempered
Khárcháṛí, cudgel
Khari hasá, chalk, (? *kari hasá*)
Kharíd ái, hedái,† purchase, buy
Khárpá, sandals, shoes
Khárrá, salted
Khársálá, pure, open, clear
Khársálá hoṛmo, fresh, active, cheerful
Khasá, brass
Khatá, master of a numerous family
Kháṭár kháṭár ái, kedái, rap, knock at, gnaw
Khaṭáu:ái, khaṭáu enái, kedái, work, labour
Kháṭí? win game or suit, gain
Khátir ái, enái, kedeái,† be pleased, agree
Kháṭo: á, enái, kedái, come short, fail, be discouraged
Kháṭo, deficiency, wanting
Khátok,† debtor

Khaṭpaṭ, cheat [ing

Khaṭpaṭí, tyranny, cheat-

Khaṭpaṭiá, fickle, unsteady, mischievous

Khaṭṭi, certainly, undoubtedly

Khaṭṭi ámái, ádeái, demand,? require? fix, determine, settle

Kháṭulṭáu ái, kedái,† upbraid for idleness

Kháuká, glutton (man)

Kháukiyá, glutton (woman)

Kháyár ? gum, catechu

Kheás ? mourn, remember the dead, think of sadly

Kheche: khechej ái, kheche: ená, kedeái, decapitate, lop off, strike off, (word derived from the sound of cutting)

Khedo:, evening meal, supper, (see *kedo:*)

Khejái ái, khejá ená, kedeái, Khejái bhejái, } divide fruit or meat &c. for sale

Kheldu ái, enái, kedeái,° play

Kheloṛo: ái, kheloṛ enái, kedeái,° perform feats in sport, play with sword, play

Khemá ? pleasure

Khemáu: ái, khemáu kedái, pass time

Khemondo: ? give pleasure

Khepáu: á, khepáu kedái, spend (time &c.) beat

Kheṛkheṛ eái, enái, kedeái, abuse, (a woman's word) scream of a cock

Kherwal, kherwar, ancient name of Sántáls

Khet,† field

Kheṭe kheṭe, laughter

Khidi bidi: á, bidi kedeái, cut into pieces, mince

Khijúr,° date tree

Khikriṉri,* a kind of fox

Khíl, ground allowed to be idle

Khílá,° wedge, pin, spike, bracelet

Khír,† rice boiled in milk, pudding

Khod, a kind of tree "jámá"

Khodá:, tattoo

Khode, grain broken fine

Khodṛáu ái, kedái, scrape off

Khog,, *ái, kho: enái, kedái*, cough

Kholáu, to hollow out, bore

Kholo,* a kind of yam

Khon, khoná: from

Khondoro,* thornbush "kirchichi"

Khontá, crowbar

Kho okhoi ái, okho enái, kedeái, hiss (as a snake), make

a noise from a concealed spot

Khorchá,° cost, expense

Khorḍá, lame

Khorogo:ái, *khoro: enái*, set teeth on edge

Khot, fertile, fertility

Khoyo, hollow

Khuchi,? a nail

Khuchilá, a kind of fish, "kunchia"

Khudáu eái, *kedeái*, pursue, drive off

Khukhi,° womb

Khulán, beauty

Khuláu,° beautiful, open-faced, to adorn, ornament

Khún,† murder, to commit murder

Khuniáhi,° murderer

Khuṇsu: khuṇsugo:ái, *khuṇsu: enái*, *kedeái*, whine, sob, sigh

Khunṭí,† post, peg, *sáte: khunṭí*, moderate sized pillar, *mutul khunṭí*, big pillar, anything built up to support a roof

Khuntut,,, stump of tree

Khuṛa,† hoof, foot

Khuṛ khuṛí, litter, palki

Khusí,† pleasure

Khusí ái, *enái*, *kedeái*,† be pleased, content, accept

Khuṭí ái, *ená*, *kedeái*, give work by job

Khuṭlái ái, *kedái*, shoot an arrow into air, spring up as water, throw up

Khuttí, a scrip for journey in which Sántáls carry cooking utensils

Khuwáu, to kill

Kíá, box for red paint

Kíchír kíchíro: á, *kíchír ená*, *kedái*, boil

Kichhu,° some, a little

Kichrí:, garment, clothes

Kichrí, clothe

Kiding, caterpillar

Kiding káṭkom, scorpion

Kiḍong hoḍong,* a kind of wild bird

Kikiáu ái, *kedái*, call out, cry bitterly, scream, make a noise

Kikir,* a kind of small red bird

Kikiṛbing,* a small water insect

Kikiṛchi: godo:ái, *got*,, *enái*, *ocho hedeái*, feel sudden fright, swoon, be numb with fear

Kil,† cork, peg

Kiláu eái, *kedeái*, punch? make holes? beat with fist

Kimin, daughter-in-law

Kinbŏkŏrŏdo: kánái, kin bokoro: enái, abuse, irritate, chatter, continue to talk after a quarrel

Kiṉrít,,, high sounding, creaking (as cart)

Kiring nái, kedeái, buy, purchase

Kiring ákring, trade, buy and sell

Kisáṉr,[o] rich, wealthy, master, owner, employer

Kiskisáu, murmur

Kisni, "*mainá*," small coloured bird

Kit,* a kind of animal

Kitá, date tree

Ko:, crane

Kobág ái, kobá: ená, kedeái, notch trees, cut a wound, make gashes (with iron) pat

Koboj,[o] possession

Koboj ái, enái, kedeái,[o] reclaim, succeed, tame animals

Kobju, stooping, bent

Kochá, corner, garden

Kocháu, accuse falsely

Kochlono:ái, kochlon enái,[o] be in pain

Kŏchŏláu,? rinse

Kochoṛ ái, kedái, hop

Kod,* a kind of flower

Kode,* millet "madwa"

Kodo: kodo:ái, enái, kedeái, curve the neck, as a sick or injured person

Koḍor ái, kedái, clean (rice, &c.) with a fan

Kohndá, a kind of fruit or vegetable, "*baitaḍ*"

Kŏhŏrái eái, kohorá ená, kedeái, fry

Koi eái, kedeái, ask, beg, entreat, pray, importune

Koilá,† charcoal, coal

Kokoli:, a sender

Kokombi:ái, enái, kedeái, have a stiff neck, lie in ambush, crouch down, look sideways without turning the body

Kokor,* a black bird of night

Kokoso:ái, kokosoi enái, kokoso kedeái, sit with clasped arms shivering

Kokoṭ ái, ená, kedái, clean land

Kol, cuckoo

Kŏl,[o] machine

Kol eái, kedeái, send, convey

Koleni:, messenger, one sent

Kŏlŏm,[o] pen

Kolsá eái, ená, kedái, push with foot

Kom,° deficient

Komáu: á, komáu enái, kedeái,° decrease

Kom idí,° diminish

Komboṛo, a thief

Komboṛoi ái, komboṛo, kedái, to steal

Komkom, sullen, sulky, have hands on the face in pain

Konách,° corner

Konḍá mánḍe: ái, mánḍe enái, kedeái, stumble, stagger as as a drunken man, roll from side to side

Kŏnḍelo: á, konḍel enái, kedeái, roll, lie down, (see *hunḍel*)

Konḍhá, crippled, maimed

Kŏnḍiá, konṛiá, konḍe: teṛhá, crooked

Kondo, fat

Koṇgneṇ, left (hand)

Konká, fool, ignorant, mad, stupid

Konká leká, foolish, stupid

Koped ái, kopet„ keḍeái, swell out the cheeks, put something in mouth

Koṛá gidirá, boy, *koṛí gidirá,* girl, maiden

Koṛá jokhai, childhood

Koṛám, breast, udder, nipple, dug, teat

Koṛám cheṭágo: ái, chetá: enái, kedeái, beat the breast

Koṛgá, blunt, turned edge

Korkot márá, peacock

Kŏrŏi: mŏtŏi:? be parsimonious, eat or live sparingly

Korṛá,° whip, scourge

Kortál, a kind of cymbal

Kosolá:ái, kosolái enái, kosolá kedeái, be in want, be in distress

Kosṭo,° affliction, distress

Kŏtábo: á, kotáp„ enái, kedeái, rap (with a stick or finger)

Koṭágo: á, koṭá: enái, hedeái, shake (clothes, feet, &c.)

Koṭá: giḍí, shake off, shake up and throw away the bad

Koṭejo: ái, koṭe: enái, kedeái, beat (with a stone or fist), bruise up

Koṭhá oṛá:, two storied house, roof

Kothráo: á, kothrá enái, kedeái, be injured, suffer loss

Koṭo, naked

Kowále, beam, rafter

Koyog„o: ái, koyo: enái, kedeái, await, gaze anxiously, expect, look up, stare, glance

Koyu, mango stone

Krús,† cross

*Kuchilá,** a kind of tree

Kuḍámrenko, neighbour's

Kudáu eái, kedeái, chase, persecute, pursue, follow (see *khudáu*)

Kuḍí,° a kind of hoe

Kuḍu, boar

Kudum, riddle, enigma

Kuduṛ kuduṛo:ái, kuduṛ enái, kedeái, be nimble, tripping (as a woman) walk lively

Kuhaṛá,° dust, fog, mist

Kuháu ái, enái, kedeái, strike with fist

Kuhnráu:ái, kuhnráu enái, kedái, sob, cry

Kuilí, a peg (of wood) wedge

Kuíṇ,† a well

*Kuinḍi,** a tree "mhowá", see also *máthom*

*Kujiri,** a kind of tree

Kukár ? smear with cow dung

Kukhí,° womb (see *khukhí*)

Kukmú, a dream

Kukmu: ái, kukmu kedái, dream

Kukṛuchu:, cockscomb

Kukṛuchug ái, kukruchu: kedái, crow, (as a cock)

Kukujo: ái, kukui: enái, kedeái, sleep with arms and legs folded in a ball, bend arm or leg

Kukuká, raise one corner of mat and cover the rice which is drying on it

Kukunáu:ái, kukunáu enái, kedái, hold urine till it is painful

Kukuku, singing of a dove

Kukute ? plaything

Kukut,, *kuḳut*,, ? dying, at point of death

Kul, kul erá, tiger, tigress

Kulạí, hare, rabbit

Kuláu ái, enái, kedeái, supply, make up deficit

Kulhí, street of a village

Kulhí daṛup, assembly, meeting, *panchayat*

Kulhí muchạt,,, just outside the village

Kuli eái, kedeái, ask, inquire, request

Kulkhí, dark or secret chamber

Kulsuring, poisonous lizard

Kulup, lock, padlock

Kulup káṭhí, key

Kúm, leathern bags in which the Mahajans carry oil

Kumá ing, m, t, my, thy, his uncle (father's sister's husband)

Kụmáu:,° want, (see *komáu*)

Kumbá, hut made of sticks,

place like an inverted V in form, shed

Kumburu ái, kedeái, rob, steal

Kukumburu: i:, robber, thief

Kumburu orá:, prison

Kumí,° want, be deficient

Kumtí idí:° decrease, diminish

Kunám,* a kind of tree

Kunámí, half moon

Kundáu: á, kundáu ená, kedái, compose, make, engrave, carve out, fashion, turn in lathe

Kundel, roll (see *kondel*)

Kunduri, kunám, a wild fruit

Kundhí, kidney of chicken

Kungkál, wasp, potter

Kunhráu:ái, kunhráu kedái, groan (in sickness)

Kunkunáu:ái, kunkunáu enái, quarrel, be angry

Kupí, earthen oil-can, vessel with small mouth

Kupuli áling, enáling, converse, ask and answer

Kuputiyá,° hypocritical

Kurá gidirá, boy, *kurí gidirá*, girl, (see *korá, korí*)

Kurai, wages

Kurámre kudámre, behind (place)

Kuráu: á, kuráu ená, kedái, suit, answer the purpose, suffice, be wanting, be deficient, be unable, be unfinished, be collected

Kurchungo:ái, kurchung enái, kedeái, limp (as dog) bend the knee (as a sleeping person)

Kurhiyá, lazy, idle

Kurit rámá, thornbush, "*kánákol*"

Kuríyá, hut

Kurkundui:, staringly

Kuromutáhá, disobliging, morose, unsocial

Kurum, sound of musical instrument, small drum

Kurumutu:ái, kurumutui enái kurumutu kedái, be active, energetic, attend diligently

Kurumutute, diligently, actively, earnestly

Kusbí,° prostitute, whore

Kusbí bahá, a kind of flower

Kustá, chaff

Kusu: kusudo:ái, kusut„ enái, kedeái, whine, sob, sigh, sniffle (see *khunsu:*)

Kutám eái, enái, kedeái, to hammer, make holes, strike with axe, hoe, &c., pierce, punch

Kutám bid„, drive in (a nail, &c.)

Kuṭám ḍángrá, sacrificial bullock

Kuṭásí, hammer

Kuṭburo:ái, kuṭbur enái, kedeái, sit with head between the knees

Kuṭháṉr, dry pieces of ground in wet fields or road, &c.

Kuṭhe, leg (of chair, table)

Kuṭhí,° storehouse

Kuṭhíl, miserly, unmerciful (only of women)

Kuṭí ái, ákáḍái, cut up, mince (meat, vegetables)

Kuṭkuṭu:ái, kuṭkuṭui enái, kutkuṭu kedeái, raise the back (as a cat)

Kuṭṛạ eái, enái, kedeái, break in pieces

Kuṭṛạ, a piece

Kyonṭá,° fisherman

L

Láb, lábh,† gain, profit

Láb ái, kedái, gain, profit

Láb ochoi, make profitable, useful

Lábạṛ, false, untrue

Lábi:, soft, mild, pliable, tender

Lábido: á, lábit„ ená, kedeái, become soft, melt a person by entreaty

Láchár,† distressed, helpless

Lád ái, lát„ kedái, roast meat, bind meat, &c. in leaves

Láde eái, ená, kedeái, bend, load, put over, put one thing on another, fall upon, spring upon

Láde jong, put on (as clothes)

Ladeá, crooked tree

Lád lád, crowds on crowds, gelatinous, thick

Láḍu, a kind of sweetmeat

Lág ái, lá: kedái, shave timber, chip wood

Lá: gulánḍ, round timber

Lagá eái, kedeái, pursue, drive off, chase

Lagá gnir, drive off or away

Lagá lagí, one after another, close together

Lagám,° saddle

Lagan bagan, trade, traffic

Lágáu ái, ená, kedeái, apply, begin, contend, vie

Lagít, lagát„, for, on account of

Lág lág chips, wood

Lágonre, a kind of bird

Lahá:ái, laháí enái, lahá kedeái, guide, send on in front, go in front

Lahánto: ái, lahá: enái, kedeái, beat, excel, surpass, guide, go in front, send on

Laháte, in front, to the front

Laháse:, in front of, before, in presence of

Laháreá kathá, prophecy

Lahár chahár, ostentation, display

Láhárá, flying clouds

Lại eái, ádeái, speak, tell, (*dat.*) tell tales of another, say, describe, direct, mention, (*acc.*)

Lại ocho, dictate

Lại báṛái, mention

Lại lábáṛ, liar

Lại ṭhík, arrange, settle

Lái:, belly, womb, bowels, entrails

Lái: oḍoko: ái, oḍok enái, have diarrhœa

Láijo: ái, lái: enái, be pregnant

Lái: látáro:, be submissive, obedient

Lái: tuliáu: fill the belly, satisfy

Lái ái, lá kedái, dig

Lá ṭánḍí, dig up

Lajáu: ái, lajáu enái, kedeái,[o] feel shame, be diffident

Lakáṛ lukuṛo:ái, lukuṛ enái, kedeái, shake from side to side, waddle, shake in the legs, tremble, be weak in feet

Lákuj ái, lákui: enái, kedeái, or ádeái, bend over, hang down

Lalá:ái, kedái, } chip, smooth,
Lá: ái, &c. } scrape

Laláu:, to suffer (pain, hunger, &c.)

Láloch,† avarice

Lálocho:ái, láloch enái, kedeái, covet, crave, long for

Lái lukṭhá:ái, lukṭhái enái, lukṭhá kedeái, contend with, pick quarrel with, annoy

Lámá:,* a kind of flower

Lámbáu: á, lámbáu ená, kedái, decay, become stale

Lámbe, 2nd crop growing of itself

Lámhám, idle

Lámpoṭ, buffoon

Lándái ái, lándá kedái, laugh

Lándái, joke

Lá: ndái:, joker

Lándái leká, absurd

Landhu ái, ená, kedái, infringe, break (order, covenant, &c.) press down, (crops, &c.) be violent, tread down

Lándŏr dhing, arrived at manhood

Lánduro: á, lándur ená, kedái, raze, demolish, tumble down

Lángá, weary

Lángá:ái, lángái enái, lángá kedái, be weary

Lángtá, naked, destitute, poor

Láng titi,* a small long-tailed bird

Lápá: chápá: á, chápái enái, chápá kedái, fall to pieces

Lapai, converse, talk together

Lapa lopo fly as young birds

Láped„ ái, lápet„ kedái, eat by morsels, take a mouthful

Láphuá, ridiculous, ludicrous, foolish

Lápichká:, corpulent woman

Lápít, barber (Hindu)

Láp lápá ái, ená kedeái, spread open (as a book, paper, cloth, &c.)

Lár, a creeper, any thing pliant, a slender snake

Lárάu: á, lárάu ená, kedeái, quake, shake, move the lips quickly, work

Larhái ái, enáling,† to fight, contend

Lárká, the Coles

Larkharáu:ái, larkharáu enái, kedái, speak fast, wish to get out words, run round and round (*e.g.*, animal in cage)

Lárkujo: á, lárkui: ená, kedái, bend a tree to get the fruit (see *lákuj„*)

Láserá:, sharp, pointed

Lásero: á, láser ená, kedái, sharpen iron, to talk fluently (as a drunken man)

Láshár,† sailor

Látárre, látárte, under, beneath

Látghát, commit fornication, copulate

Lathá, birdlime

Láthe, a kind of fruit-tree

Látíjo:ái, láti: kedái, bend the body back by shoulders so as to make the chest protrude

Latpat, roll (in the mud, &c.)

Látpatáu,° faint (from hunger, sickness, &c.)

Látu látu, round (as fruit)

Látum ái, kedái, devour, swallow up greedily

Láṭumo:ái, láṭum ená, kedái, seize, double, fold up

Lauka,[o] boat

Láuṭá, snare for birds

Láwero:ái, láwer ená, kedeái, bend, incline

Leá ená, kedái, wash away as by a flood, crumble away, melt, dissolve, fall to dust or powder

Leáu, play, sport

Lebdái ái, lebdá kedeái, cast (a net), throw, throw away

Lebedo:ái, lebet„ kedeái, kick, press down

Le: bedá gándo, footstool

Lebet„ gásmándáu: á, gásmándáu ená, kedeái, tread under foot

Lebṛá, glutton, covetous

Leche leche,? unequal? uneven? unsteady, as a man carrying a heavy weight

Lechej„ ái, leche: enái, kedái, winnow, throw up grain in fan to sift it

Ledám,? edge

Leḍhá:ái, leḍhái enái, leḍhá kedeái, be lame, limp

Leḍhí, lame (woman)

Leg, fit, suitable, proper, custom, right, due

Lego:ái, leg kedái, act properly, act according to custom

Lege: lábágo: á, lábá: ená, kedái, be tender, be verdant, be soft (as grass)

Lege: lege:, tender, green, &c. (grass)

Lege: legejo: á, lege: enái, kedái, be green, be flourishing

Legem legem, softly, gently

Legesá:, fat, plump (as children)

Lek,[o] worthy

Lekte,[o] worthily

Leká, like

Leká ái, kedái, liken

Lekhái ái, ená, kedeái,[o] count, reckon, esteem, deem, add up, consider, resemble

Lekhá jokhái,[o] keep accounts

Lekhá,[o] a number

Lelhá, lelhí, foolish (man, woman) blockhead, dunce

Lelenge:, smooth, placid, distant object, indistinct

Lemeng, powder

Lemeng lemeng nái, ená, kedái, pulverize

Lemlem, gently, gracefully

Lemṭo:, unripe, tasteless

Len ái, ená, kedeái, squeeze out, express (oil, &c.), press

Leno: páṭá oil press

Lendá, sediment, dregs, very small

Lenḍe:, earthworm

Lende mochá:,? nearly ripe

Lengá, left hand or foot

Leng chalá:, crawl along (as a snake)

Lenge: lengedo: ái, lenget,, enái kedeái, be in danger

Lengnedo:
Lenjedo:ái, lenjet,, enái, kedeái, } slip, slide

Lenjer, lenjet, slippery, greasy, polished, muddy

Leohái ái, ená, kedái, mix, stir up

Lepen tepen, piled up, irregular, rabble, crowd

Leper leper, paste, starch, mud and water

Lepe: teṛel, a kind of tree "kendu"

Lere,? expedient, plan, means

Lesáṉrhe:, to come with false pretences

Lesej,, ái, lese: kedeái, snap, snarl

Lesen, to knock over by foot

Lese pese: á, lese pese ená, kedái, make mud, become muddy

Lesker, fat (as pigs)

Letej ái, lete: kedái, accomplish purpose, perform successfully

Leṭep,, leṭep,,, lifeless, half dead

Leṭe peṭe, mudlike, rice cooked into a paste

Lethá,? children

Libir libir, soft, flabby as earth after rain, or leather when wet

Lichaṛ,° weak, helpless

Likit,, likido: á, likit,, ená, kedái, swing in the wind, shake about (as branch)

Lál,° indigo

Lílám,° a sale, auction

Lílámo:, have a sale or auction

Limbodo:ái, limbot,, ená, kedeái, strangle, be strangled

Lin ái, kedeái, pinch, catch tight, hold by a gripe

Linḍaro: ái, linḍar enái, kedeái, attend to business, be skilful, clever, be well accquainted with

Lindi, fundament

Lindi eái, kedeái, mock

Linjido: á, linjit" ená, kedái, flow in drops, run gently, trickle

*Lipi,** a kind of small bird

Lipindhi, glistening, shining, glittering, as crystal

Lip lip, clear, transparent, burnished

Lipsá, limber, pliant

Lipúr lipúr, tinkling, a jingling instrument bound on hands, feet or wrist

Liṛi:, child, small

Liṛi: gidirá, baby

Lísind ái, kedái, hunt for a fault, seek occasion against, exaggerate evil

Líṭa, rainbow

Liṭí:, to decay, become bad, (as meat, rice, &c.), rot

Liwá liwi:, to bob about

Liwedo: á, liwet" enái, kedeái, bend down

Lo:ái, lo ená, kedái, burn

Lobdháu:ái, lobdháu enái, kedeái, be surprised, charmed, delighted

Lobh ái, kedái,° covet

Lobhátíyá,? covetous

Lobháu eái, enái, kedeái, seduce, amuse, divert

Lobo: lobo:,? jolt? jerk? stout

Lobo: muiṇ, red ant (very small)

Locháí ái, lochá kedái, eat (with hands) put hand into dish

Lopochá, eat together off one plate

Lo dá:, su: dá:, well, a small hole in sand near a river

Lodám, a kind of tree, first step on a hill, rising ground at foot of hills

Logon, marriage ceremonies, dance (at weddings)

Lohot", wet

Lohodo:ái, lohot" ená, kedeái, to wet

Loi ái, lo kedái, draw water, strain off water

Loi:, penis

Lokái ái, loká kedeái, toss up and catch

Lokáu,? bend

Loktá, connexion, "bát," quarrel, dispute

Lolo, hot, warm

Lomor, snout (of animals)

Lonboni:, agent, one who carries on work for another

Lonḍo lonḍo, staring intently

Lonká, lonkí, man or woman weak in arms

Lopong, a tree

Loṛáu:ái, loṛáu enái, kedeái, faint, become weak, be worn out, be hungry and thirsty

Loṛe, a kind of creeper? (met.) *kathá loṛe en táiá* "his word was proud"

Loṛoyo, dunce, silent

Loság ái, losá: kedeái, snap, snarl, be angry

Loso ponḍo:ái, ponḍoi enái, ponḍo kedeái, be muddy, be dusty, roll in the dirt

Lŏsŏt, mud, dirty

Loṭghoṭi ái, kedái, commit fornication, be quarrelsome, injure one's property

Lŏṭŏi:, large fly

Loṭojo:ái, loṭoi: enái, kedeái, strain, sprain, hang down (as a half broken branch), bend

Lŏṭŏm ái, ená, kedeái, deny, silence (another) overcome (habits, &c.) press down

Lowá, kind of fig-tree "dumbal"

Luchá, exacting, exorbitant

Luchá lámot,,, lustful, avaricious

Lugṛí, cloth, *dhotí*

Luiyut,, luiyut,,, aghast, astonished, very frightened, startled, coward

Lukní, a coarse grass

Lulhạ, wrist, hand from the wrist

Luṭhu:, successful player? the odd man at a game, a play

Luṭí, lips

Luṭkurí,? side of face

Lutur, ear

Lutur bhugá:, orifice of the ear

Lutur peṭer, to rub the ear (box ears)

Lutur bíd, erect the ear, listen

Lutur oḍáu, put hand to ear (as a person does who strives to hear)

Lutur hupạ, part of face just below the ears

M

Machhá, somewhat, like

Máchhi, border of a cloth

Máchi, chair, stool, rice-water?

Machháu:ái, machháu ená, kedái, / *Maṛkáu:,* be sprained

Madwáte, small pox

Mág,, eái, má: ená, kedái, cut, attack, assault, chop

Má: giḍi, amputate

Má: ṭánḍí, clear land

Mápág„ áling, mápá: enáling, fight, mutually cut

Má: goje ái, má: goi: enái, kedeái, kill by sword

Má: duṛup, wound

Máhákáu: á, máhákáu enái, kedeái, stink

Mahán̩, day

Mahán̩der, day before yesterday

Máhará, shepherd, cowherd

Mahárog,† plague, famine

Máhíkal,* a kind of bird

Máhimá,† glory, greatness

Máhír, abstinent, soft, temperate, gentle, compassionate, kind, gentleness

Máhíro:ái, máhír enái, kedeái, be gentle

Mahjíd,^o mosque

Máhkálom, three years ago

Máhrog, precious, valuable, costly, dear

Máhúr, poison

Máijiu, woman, wife

Mailá,† filth

Maiṇg, said to a daughter

Makordamá,^o affair

Mákú, shuttle for weaving, word used to call a sister

Mál,† goods, wealth, property

Málá,† string of beads

Málí, oil vessel, little lamp, gardener

Málí bahá, a kind of red flower

Málkáu:ái, málkáu enái, kedái, be wanton, glisten, lighten, shine, be ostentatious

Málkáute, vainly

Málungo:ái, málung enái, kedeái, be astonished, delighted

Mámbṛá: mámbṛi:, pushing, jostling, shoving, pulling

Mán,^o a measure of 80lbs.

Mạn, land received without rent for office-work done, as *manjhi, goret*, &c.

Maná eái, kedái,† forbid, prohibit, hinder

Mánán ái, ádeái, kedái,† sacrifice, vow in sickness, &c., a vow

Manáu eái, enái, kedeái,^o love, regard, assent to, obey

Manḍái ái, manḍá ená, kedái, thresh

Mándán bheḍ, the large Sántál trumpet

Mándár gom, custard apple

Mánde, rubbish, heaps of filth, dunghill

Mandilá táká, the marriage rupee given to the *mánjhí* of bride's village

Mandir,† temple

Mándrau: ái, mandrau enái, fly over or about, hover, whirl

Manduá, shed erected in bride's village where the rice and *sendur* are buried at a marriage

Mángníte, freely, without price

Mangrá,† tiles on top of roof

Mángrí,* a kind of fish

Mángrí gocho, moustache

Manjái ái, ená, kedái, scrub, clean, scour

Mánján, middle day meal, dinner

Mánjhí, the headman of a [village

Mánot,° dignity, grandeur

Mánrángre, mánrángte, before (time)

Mánrángreá kathá, prophecy

Manrí, corpse

Mánrom, sheds on which the Sántáls keep their straw

Mánsí,? pith of a tree

Mántár,† a charm

Mántár ái, kedái,† charm

Mámú ing, (*m.t.*), my, thy, his uncle (mother's brother)

Mánwá,° human being, mankind, men

Mánwí jánám,° human, human race

Mápánji, *punchayat* of the *manjhis* of several villages

Mápit,,, *mápík*,° like, according to

Mára:, peacock

Matu mára:, peahen

Máráng, great, large, big

Máráng engáing, engám, engát, my, thy, his aunt (wife of father's eldest brother)

Máráng ájing, eldest sister

Máráng dádá, dádám, dádát, my, thy, his (eldest) brother

Máráng burú, God, demon, Satan

Máráng dukh, plague, pestilence

Máránr bahá,* tree with large red flowers

Márár, yoke

Maráu: ái, maráu ená, kedái,° die away, fade, be abolished, wear off (as shame, fear, &c.)

Márchá, worn out, uncultivated, running to weed, exhausted (as ground)

Máre, ancient, old

Marí,† plague

Marí gutí, small-pox

Maṛí, corpse, carcase, carrion (see also *maṉṟí*)

Maṛí gaḍá, *maṛí ṭháṇw*, *maṛí oṛá:*, grave

Marjạd,⁰ honour, reverence, renown

Maṛkáu, sprain (see *machkáu*)

Mársál, light, clean, white

Mársálo:ái, *mársál ená*, *kedeái*, give light, be clean

Mársálte, brightly

Mashúṛá, wisdom tooth

Másrá,? monthly

Másúl,⁰ custom, tax

Mát,? sow first seed of the season

Mát„, bamboo

Mát„ *ḍáng*, grove of bamboos

Mát oṛá:, temple, church

Mátá mátur,? destitute, forsaken

Mátáleá,⁰ drunkard

Mátkom, a kind of tree, "mhowá"

Máṭmáṭáu:ái, *máṭáu enái*, grin, fix the teeth (sound from the noise of the teeth) eat something hard

Máyá,† pity, mercy

Máyá:ái, *máyá enái*, *ádeái*,† sympathize, feel pity, feel mercy

Máyám, blood

Máyám oḍok, bleed, have dysentery

Máyo, woman, coward

Me:, the eye

Me: kuṭí, eyebrows, the whole hollow formed by the eye

Me: do, *meṇdo*, eye disease, ophthalmia

Me: te, as far as eye can see

Met„ *áháṇ*, face

Me: dá:, tear

Me: dá: joro:, shed tears

Met„ *áenomo:ái*, *áenom kedái*, paint round the eyes

Me: jápido:ái, *jápit*„ *enái*, *kedeái*, close the eyes

Me: jolo:, be envious

Me: me: gnepel, interview

Me: bajáu:, cast eye upon

Meáng, day after to-morrow

Mechká mechkí, wanton, making a set at a man, shaking the head to attract attention

Meheṇ,? threshing-floor

Mehuṇ, calf

Mehuṇ merom, cattle (liter. calves and goats)

Mej,† table

Melá, melán, open, unenclosed, clear, wide, extended

Men ái, kedái, met ádeái, to say

Men jong, desire, wish, suppose

Mená:, it is

Menáko hoṛ, some men

Menek, nevertheless, but, still

Menkhán, but

Meṉrheṇt, iron, steel

Mente, on account of, for, in order that

Merá, refuse of "mhowá" after distilling

Meráye:, unavailing, fruitless, useless

Merlei:,* a thorny tree

Merom, goat

Merom me:, a kind of tree

Mesál eái, ená, kedái, add, mix

Mesál misi, in confusion, mixed

Met, call, bid (see *men*)

Metá:, called, viz., named

Metáme, grant

Metáu giḍi,⁰ par don

M:i, one, a, alike, similar, resembling

Mimi:, every one, each, one by one

Mimit„ mimit„ te, one at a time, one by one

Mit„ hoṇ mit„, every single one

Mi: tigi, mi: te, altogether, together

Mi: sing mi: gnindá, all day and night

Mi: sámán, mi: sáuṇ, even, level

Mi: dháute, mi: dháu, mi: chhot, once

Mi: pis,? one sided

Mi: ṭhen, in one place, together

Mi: tur, of one thickness, one layer

Mi: jomkáu, unanimous

Mi: taláu, uniformly, continually

Mi: jok, level, even, of one size

Mido:, mit„ ocho, to mix, mingle, resemble, unite

Mi: monte, sincerely, heartily

Mi: barábarí, resembling, alike, similar

Mi: kathá, faithful to one's word, agree together

Mi: ghoṛíte, at once, quickly

Mi: ghoṛí khái: gi, after a short time

Mi: ṭung, the slightest, the smallest [wife)

Mi: jiṅi, one souled (of a

Mi: mohndáte, straight ahead

Mi: lái: ren, brother

Mi: sir, eunuch

Mi: bár dháu, occasionally

Mi: kár goi: ákán hoṛ, paralytic

Mi: rogoṛte, uniformly

Michhạ, in vain, falsely, contemptible worthless

Michhạgi met, despise

Milág,? join, splice

Mil julo:ái, jul ená, kedeái, to live on friendly terms

Mili misi, mili guti, plot, scheme

Miloá enái, kedeái, commit adultery, &c.

Miloá ghaṭá, fornication, adultery

Mirju bahá,* a kind of flowery tree

Mirlung, humbly

Mirú, a parrot

Mís, to plot, conspire, hold secret counsel

Mísá:, plot, conspiracy

Misí ái, kedeái, paint the teeth, blacken

Misrit„ ái, ená, kedái, fix (upon a plan) settle, determine, arrange

Míṭhái,† sweet meats

Mithí sunum,[o] a kind of oil made of *mithí* to be rubbed on body

Mo:ái, mo ená, kedeái, swell

Mochá, face, mouth

Mochá lin, put hand on another's mouth to prevent speaking

Mocholká ái, enái, ocho kedeái, make agreement, covenant

Mochṛáu, twist

Mohjor, difficult, hard

Mohṉdá, appearance, direction

Mohṉdá:ái, mohndá ená, kedeái, face, be turned towards

Mohṉdá mohṉdí, face to face [wards

Mi: mohndáte, straight to-

Mohokubo: á, mohokúp„ ená, kedái,[o] suspend, abolish, forbid

Mŏhŏr meṭáu ái, ená, kedái, destroy, die, wipe out, disappear, abolish

Moká, cubit

Mo: kisni,? toadstool

Mokoingno:ái, mokoing enái, complete, finish, be satisfied, have enough

Moláu, mortgage

Molong, forehead

Molong áni:, fortunate

Molong tupuingno: ákin, tupuing enákin, beat the forehead mutually

Momoyut,,, ashamed, sorrowful (applied to a person discovered in a fault)

Mon,[o] mind, heart

Mon khát̤o:ái, enái, ocho kedeái, be sorrowful, depressed

Mŏndá, the Coles

Mon̤dá: á, mon̤dá enái, kedái, spoil by keeping, become bad

Mŏne ái, kedái,[o] think, wish, intend, desire

Mŏne,[o] mind, choice, wish, desire, soul

Mŏne rebed,,, to love

Mŏne achur, repent

Mŏne gad̤áu or *urij,,*, apply oneself heartily, be diligent

Mŏn gad̤áu, pleasing

Mŏne heju:, come to mind, occur

Mŏnechŏng, what, indeed

Mon̲j, mon̲ják,,, good, good-looking, good to talk, beautiful, pretty

Mon̲reko turuiko, one of the Sántál gods (*lit.*, the fives and sixes)

Morá, thin, lean, feeble, weak, powerless

Mor̤ái, increase in size (as growing rice)

Morá muhán̲r, the south, the point to which the Sántáls turn when burying their dead

Moron,[o] death

Mosodo: á, mosot,, ená, kedái, fade away (as trees, &c.), wither

Mosolá,[o] spices

Moste, see "muste"

Mot̤á,† fat, bass voice

Mot̤á anjom, hear with difficulty

Mot̤á ruar̤o:, become strong again, fat after sickness

Mot̤ge, by force, tyrannically, oppressively

Mot̤ sáp, compel to do work

Mot̤rá,[o] bundle

Moṭrá juṭrái ái, / *moṭrá juṭrá ená* / *kedái,* } goods and chattels, parcels and pack

Moṭyám, seize, grasp, take

Muchạt, top, end, the back part

Muchạtre, finally

Muchhí huṛú, black rice

Muchí,° drum makers (a caste)

Muchu, open basket (for fishing)

Muckur muchur jom, to munch, eat, make noise in eating

Mudá,? stolen goods

Muḍu lái: small entrails

Mug,* a kind of pulse

Muhin, *muhim*, risk, danger, affliction

Muiṇ ant

Muiṇ leká, crowded

Mukhạrat,° face to face

Mukhiyá,† chief, principal person

Muktáu:, be full

Muktí,† pearl

Mukulte,? perform ceremonies after childbirth

Mul ái, *ená*, *kedái*,† appraise, value, appoint, fix, settle, give pattern

Mule habádo: á, *habát*,, *kedái*, destroy

Mulíno:ái, *mulín enái*, *kedeái*,° be sorrowful, sad

Mul, *mur*,† pattern, original. primary

Mului: mului:, a smile

Muṇ,° nose

Muṇ bhugạ:, nostrils

Muṇd, among

Mundáu: á, *mundáu enái*, *kedeái*, close up (hole, &c.), close in, join

Muṇdhát,, logs, blocks of wood

Muṇdoi,° plaintiff

Muṇḍrá,° shaved head

Muṇḍu, jungle

Munís, servant

Múṉrdám? *muṇdám*, *mudám*, ring

Murdí, crib, manger, granary, "tek"

Murchháu: á, *murchháu ená*, *kedái*,° rust, corrode, square the end of a log, smooth with adze, &c.

Murgá, a kind of tree, "piasal"

Murhui: jom, leprosy

Murhui: jomi:, leper

Murhut,,° image, idol

Muru:, a kind of tree

Murúbe,° aged man, elder

Muruko:ái, *muruk enái*, *ocho*

kedeái, be attentive, apply diligently, lean against, press against
Muskíl,° arduous, difficult
Mussá, silent
Muste em, lend, have for nothing, receive for nothing
Muṭo:ái, muṭ kedái, draw a sword, catch hold as one would of a sword, grasp
Mutak, staff, thick stick
Muthá, a low kind of grass
Muṭhạn, image, appearance
Muthní, summit, top, peak
Mutul kátup middle finger
  Mutul khunṭí, longest and middle pillars of a house

N

Nabí,† prophet
Náchu, a basket placed to catch fish
Nádo:,? to practise austerities
Nafá,† advantage
Nagráhá, nangráhá,° city
Nahá:, now
  Nahá: jug, the present time
Náhak,° worthless, in vain
  Nahaká:,° vanity
Nahel, plough
  Nahel gáṛá or *gaḍá,* furrow
Naí, the Damoda River into which the Sántáls throw their dead
Náib,† deputy
Náikki, Sántál priest
Náiṉnu, butter
Nakhá, side
Náki:, a comb
  Nákíjo:ái, náhí: kedeái, comb
Naksá,° drawing, picture
Nálá,† channel, ditch, drain
Nálhá, wages, food for work
  Nálhá jong, make a livelihood
Nális ái, ená, ádeái,° complain, have a lawsuit
Námdák,° well-known, notorious, celebrated, renowned
Nána hunạr,° different kinds
Nánḍá, nánrá, some rice left in the field for the poor
Nangá,° devotee
Nángŏs ái, kedái, pretend
Nangráhá,° city, bazaar (see also *nagráhá*)
Nánhá, thin, fine, nice, slight, slender (as a stick, &c.)
Nanjom, witch
Nanrí, a creeper (plant)

Nápáio:, be established, be settled, be good, be clean

Nápái okoi:, very good

Napṛá:, great, large

Nari,† pulse

*Náṛi chaaṛá,** a kind of vegetable

Naṛ joṛo: ákin, jor enákin, ket kinái, marry

Nárkoṛ, cocoa nut

Narṛi, throat

Náse, false, light, foolish, vain, a little

Náse seturá, thoughtless, vain, giddy

Nátikár, koṛáring erá, granddaughter

Náti koṛáring, grandson

Naṭwá, to reel silk

Nán'án, fresh, new, recent

Náuṇ, barber

Nawágṇi, to offer in sacrifice, present firstfruits

Ne, take (imperative); *neho*, to a man; *neyáṇ*, to a child

Ne betár, now, these times

Nee, this indeed

Ne párom, this side

Ne nahá:, now, immediately

Neáo,° to decide, determine, settle

Neḥado:ái, neḥaṭ„ enái, kedeái, be little, small, despised

Nehoro:ái, nehor enái, kedeái, be zealous, be earnest, beseech, entreat, ask earnestly, pray, importune

Nehot eái, ená, kedeái, press down, disobey (a command), deny, despise, contemn

Neṇḍá, covenant, agreement, arrangement, stipulated

Nenkán, thus

Neotá eái, kedeái,† invite, give a feast.

Nes, this year

Niá, this (neut.)

Nichhurá, spotless, quite clean

Níchind, unawares, ignorant

Níchŏl, desolate, lonely, solitary

Nídandi, safe, secure, unconcerned

Nidharúá, rich, free from debt

Níhaṭ eái, ená, kedeái, think small of, despise, scorn [see also *neḥado:*]

Nihaṭge, very little

Nijáu:ái, nijáu enái, kedái, be recovering from drunkenness, get well by medicine

Níjhúm, lonely, solitary, calm, still

Níjor,° weak, weakness

Níjrúá, hale, well

Nikhaṛ ái, enái, kedeái, get perfectly well, to recover entirely

Ním, a kind of tree, "ním"

Nimbrot eái, enái, kedeái, soften, appease, be reconciled

Níṇa:, nínáng, niṇa: báṛe, } so
„ *níṇa: ge*
many, so, thus much or many

Níndáu,° to slander

Níṇdhán, gentle, low, small

Niṇghá, axletree

Niphuṭ, hale, well, pure, sinless, unmixed, unbroken, unarmed, one of a pair when the mate has died, *e.g.* one bullock

Nirá,† pure, unmixed

Nirá mone, pure-minded, singleminded

Nirbáh,† daily fare

Nirbudh,° ignorant, stupid

Nirghin, disfigured through sorrow, heart struck

Niron, warmth, sunshine

Niron din, summer

Nistár,† salvation, deliverance

Nísún,° empty, void, desolate, deserted

Nít, níto, níto do, nítgi, nít báṛe, now

Nít hábí:, until now

Nit sahí,? exact, true

Niurá,? anklet

Noláu: á, noláu ená, kedeái, prepare, investigate, examine

Nŏnḍe, here, in this place

Nŏnḍená, of, or belonging to, this place

Nŏnká, nŏnkán, so, thus

Nonkáte, in this manner

Nonkái ái, nonká ená, kedái, do so

Nonkán ái, be so

No párom, this side

Nŏsíb,° fate, fortune

Nosíb ánái, fortunate

Nosṭo eái, enái, kedeái, destroy, annihilate

Nŏte, here, hither

Noteá, a call to any one

Notená, the (things) of this side

Núá, núi, this, it, this person

Nuá hábi:, until now

Nuáte, therefore, whereupon, on this, for this reason

Nuṇa, nun, so much, so many

Nunaṇg, thus much

Nuṇa habi: insomuch, so that

Nun máráng, thus big

Nunu áiái ádeái, suckle, nurse

Nyút, dark, darkness

Nyúto: á, nyút enái, kedeái, become dark, be benighted

O

O:, smoke

O: á, o: ená, kedeái, to smoke

O: goje:, to suffocate by smoke

Oár, deliverance, salvation

Oáris, helper, saviour

Oáro:ái, oár ená, kedeái, extricate, deliver, rescue

Ochŏg,, o:ái, ocho: ená, kedeái, clear the way, remove, take away, transfer to another place

Ochut,,, hump of bull, fireplace

Odá, wetted

Odám, otter

Oḍáu ái, ená, kedeái, spread out

Oḍo: á, oḍ ená, kedeái, shelter, protect, defend

Oḍoko:ái, oḍok ená, kedeái, come or go or bring out, extract, expel

Oḍung, come out

Ofsor,° opportunity, leisure, means [See also *afsor*]

Ogher,? be insensible

Oho, What a pity!

Ohŏráu: á, ohoráu ená, kedái, assuage, decrease, become gradually silent, lessen, abate, diminish

Ojhá, doctor, physician, teacher of charms

Ojo, boil, abscess

Ojogo:ái, ojo: ená, kedeái, grease, rub on oil, &c.

Oká, what

Oká leká, in what way, how

Oká se:, where, whither, in what direction or side

Oká khon, whence

Oká hilo:, oká ghoṛi, when, what time

Oká ṭhenre, in what place, in the place which

Oká te, whither

Okáṭá te, in what, wherever

Oká re, where, anywhere

Okáre hoṇ báng, nowhere

Oká báte, how quickly!

Oká tehoṇ, by any means

Okáte hoṇ báng, by no means

Oká do, occasionally

Oká bhạgte, uncertainly, with difficulty, who knows how

Oko:ái, okoi ená, kedeái, hide, conceal (also *okun* in present and future tenses)

Okore, privately, secretly

Okun ṭhen, a hiding-place

Okoe, who

Okoi:, many (in comp.); as *aḍí okoí:*

Oktá mángál, a reproach, bye-word

Oktáu áiái, ádeái, despise, slander, spread reports, tell tales

Okte machhá, season, the proper season

Okte okte,° at times, at proper seasons

Ol: writing

Olo: á, ol kedái, to write, draw (pictures), spoil, become bad, fade, dry, wither (as leaves), be musty

Olá:, written paper

Ol bándhi,? arrest

O:oli:, a writer, an author

Oláng-mocháng, greedy, pick-pocket, thievish (particularly used of cattle)

Oloingno:ái, oloing enái, kedeái, be troubled, cast down, frightened, sad, sorrowful

Olŏm jhŏlŏm, finery, ornaments

Ombágo:ái, ombá: enái, kedeái, kneel

Omono: á, omon ená, kedái, germinate, spring forth (as seeds), shoot out, be born

Oná, that (thing)

Oná leká, onkáge, like that, in that manner, &c.

Onágese, onechŏng, that indeed

Oná hoṇ, that even, that also

Oná te, oná mente / *Oná teráng* } therefore, for that cause, whereupon, at this

Oná maháṇder, three days ago

Onḍe, there, that place

Onḍgá, those who sacrifice human beings, "Thugs"

Ong ái, kedái, blow

Ongsŏng, friendship, peace, friend

On jolo:,° to eat and drink, to take refreshment

Onmán ái, kedái, investigate, perceive, discover

On párom, that side

Onŏl gŏnŏl, checked, checquered
Onte, thither
Onte nŏte, hither and thither
Onte note: áko, note enáko, ketkoai, scatter
Ontor,° heart
Opát,,, young tree (very small)
Opŏr áling, ená, pull in different directions
Opor jopor chalá:, to follow close upon, be hard upon
Oṛá:, house, dwelling
Oṛág ái, oṛá: enái, kedái, make a house, dwell, inhabit
Oṛá: grosti ko, members of a family
Orá parí, turn and turn about
Ordá:, snare birds
Oṛe, quail
Oṛejo:ái, oṛe: enái, kedái, burst, rend, tear, tear in pieces
Oṛe: háting, split into half
Oṛe:, rent, fissure, gap
Oṛheṇo:ái, oṛheṇ enái, kedeái, praise, recount deeds, celebrate fame
Oṛlo, dull, silly, stupid, ignorant, obtuse, fool
Oṛmŏi:, bug
Oro:ái, or ená, kedeái, draw, pull, drag with the hands
Or asid, to tie in a slip knot
Oroch,? want of appetite
Oroj,° petition, request
Orojo:ái, oroj kedái, beseech, apply, make request
Orong ái, kedái, play, blow an instrument
O:rongi:, musician
Orop koṭop,* a wild esculent root
Ortáb ái, ortáp,, *ená, kedeái*, draw through
Orwál,† awning, screen, veil for women, a kind of bird
Osár, wide, extended, broad
Osogo:ái, oso: enái, kedeái, worn out, thin (from sickness)
Oso: koti, become thin
Osoráu, to begin, prepare
Ot,, *kisni, ot*,,, toadstool, mushroom
Ot,, *gopá:* } different
Ot,, *dá: mánde* } kinds of mushrooms
Ot, world, earth
Ot ot te, on foot, by land
Ot hiláu:, earthquake
Oṭágo: á, oṭá: ena, kedái, open (a book), uncover

Oṭángo:ái, oṭáng ená, kedeái, winnow by letting the grains fall about, fly, throw up in air, dissipate, squander

Otet,[m] valley

Otong eái, kedeái, follow, chase

Otong táyom, one after another, in turn, before and after, order, caste, successful

Otoṛo: á, otoṛ ená, kedeái, raze, break down (house, fence, &c.)

Oyo:ái, oyoi enái, oyo kedeái, wrap one's self up, clothe one's self

O yo: á:, oyoná:, garments, vestments

Oyŏng ái, kedeái, peep, look down upon, stoop to look

Oyug ái, oyu: enái, kedeái, strike with sword, be born

P

Päág dŏn, sword dance

Pách,? bleed, let blood

Pacháu: á, pacháu ená, kedái,[o] digest food

Pachhái ái, pachhá kedái, lay hold of a fault, reckon, consider, find out

Pachhim,† west

Páchil,[o] load a cart too heavily behind, walk backwards

Pachilá, binder part of a cart

Pachilạ enái, pạch kedeái, walk backwards

Pachnáu:ái, pachnáu enái, kedeái, recognise

Pachrí, fence, enclosure, hedge

Pachrí achur, fortify, enclose a village by earth, &c.

Paḍhua,? sluggard

Páerá ái, kedái, swim

Páerá baṛái, wander about be a vagabond

Págur ái, kedái, chew the cud

Pahá poho, dawn

Páhil,[o] first

Páhiláunṭá, firstborn

Páhilre, first, before, in advance, already, anciently

Pahṭá, piece, strip, division

Páhuṛ, sacrifice

Pạihạ, follower, pupil, disciple

Páik,? messenger

Páilá, a measure about one quart

Páinchí, long pieces of cloth (as *dhotis, chaddars*, &c.)

Páingán, anklet with bells (put on at dances, &c.)

Páisá,† pence, coppers, money
Pájhár, kite
Páji,° scoundrel
Pakáre,* a kind of tree
Pakhá, shelf, niche
Páktá,?° ripe, cooked, grown to maturity, full grown
Pál, ploughshare
Pálá,° power, authority, control, state
Pálák, bed, cot
Pálák párkom, a large kind of bed
Pálång, saddle of a horse or ox
Pálång ái, kedái, spread out,? put on a saddle
Palá: pologo: á, polo: enái, to be dim (as the eye)
Páláṭo:ái, pálát enái, kedeái, change clothes
Pálo: á, páloi ená, pálo kedái, grow white (as drying leaves)
Pán,† betel "pán"
Pán rán, medicine
Pánáhi, shoes, slippers
Pánchá em, lend, advance money for a short time
Panchí, small and light *chaddar*
Pánde, groin
Pánḍit,† learned
Pándolo:ái, pándol ená, kedeái, miss a chance, beat, surpass, excel, conquer, defeat, push away, overcome, press down
Pándráhi, filthy, disgusting, dirty, untidy, uncleanly
Panḍu: á, panḍui ená, panḍu kedai, become grey or hoary, wither, dry as leaves
Panḍu úp, white hair
Pánjá, footprint
Pánjái eái, pánjá ená, kedeái, trace, pursue, track, follow, search, leave footmarks
Panjá tiog,,, overtake
Panjár, rib
Panjrí, frame of cart, the pieces of wood put crossways in a native *gáṛí*
Pánk, bottom of river
Pánmuhiri,* spices, "sonp"
Pánte: ále, pánte enále, ket koái, sit or walk in a row
Pánṭilo:ái, pánṭil enái, kedái, bound off, spring up, jump up
Panwár gocho, whiskers
Páp,† sin
Pápi, sinful
Páṛá,? cockfighting-place
Páṛá:, rent, crack (in wood ground, &c)

Paṛá: chhirchatur, split into pieces

Paṛágo: á, paṛá: ená, kedái, split, rend, divide

Párágáṛe, overhear,? spy,? discover secretly, wander about saunteringly

Parámáp,? bespeak

Parámes,?° to advise, consult

Parámánik, prime minister of the *mánjhi*, second man in the village

Páṛáu: á, páṛáu ená,° be, fall, obtain

Paráunchá, stands on which the Sántáls keep their straw

Párcháu: á, parcháu ená, kedái, be plentiful (as flowers) spread, increase

Párgáná, chief Sántál officer, with from twenty to sixty villages under him

Parháu ái, kedeái, read, study

Pári-párite, take by, or in, turns

Pári ruạ, intermittent fever

Pariạ, time, generation

Páris, generation, tribe, caste, family

Párkom, bed, cot

Paṛlak, stripe on the borders of a cloth

Párlek, almost, perhaps, possibly

Párom, over, beyond

Páromo:ái, párom ená, kedeái, cross over, convey over [through

Párom chalá:, pass by, or

Pársi, phársi, language

Párwá, dove

Pásáro: á, pásár ená, kedái, fly open, spread out

Páse, parlek, if, lest

Pasí:, net for birds

Pasí:ái, pasí enái, kedeái, catch or be caught, entrap, catch in talk, find out

Pásiro: á, pásir ená, kedái, scatter, fly about, rebound, fly off as chips

Páskái ái, páská kedái, scrape with the foot

Paskáu, escape, slip away (see *phaskáu*)

Pásnáu:á, pásnáu ená, kedái, spread, be or make known, circulate, publish, scatter

Pásuṛo:ái, pásuṛ enái, kedeái, slip away, let slip, work in vain

Pátá, board, slate

Páṭáhárháng,* a spotted poisonous snake

Pátái ái, pátá enái, kedái, swing on hooks (as devotees)

Pátáṛá:, split wood

Patár patár, to gnaw

Pátáṛ potoṛ, bush, bushes, shrubs

Páṭár poṭor, hairless, featherless (used of birds, animals), destitute of grass

Páṭáu ái, hedái, level floor by pounding, smear floor, water flowers

Páṭchelá, scholar, one who lives with a *guṛú*

Páṭgánḍo:ái, gánḍoi enái, gánḍo kedeái, sit on ground with legs crossed

Páṭh,† lesson, reading task

Páthá, páṭhí,† kid (male and female), lamb,? pig?

Páṭhe:ái, páṭhe enái, kedeái, bind clothes tight, gird the loins

Pathrí, the art of throwing charms known to "ojhas" by which the person thrown at dies, ejecting spittle at a person

Páṭí ái, ená, kedeái, bore, make a hole, prick

Paṭiá, mat (made of palm leaves)

Patiáu:ái, patiáu enái, hedái, believe, credit, have faith, feel confidence

Páṭiháro:ái, paṭihár enái, kedeái, draw blood from one's body as the Sántál "gurus" do

Páṭi jilád eái, jilát,, ená, kedeái, nail up, fix, fasten

Páṭhá, tough

Patṛá, flat plate of leaves

Páṭsir,? heel ropes

Paṭṭá, old, tough (as chicken), rotten (as meal, &c.), lease

Páṭṭá sákám,[o] lease

Páṭub ái, páṭup,, enái, kedeái, root out, tear up by roots, lever up

Páṭwet,,, deceitful, crafty

Paurá, a liquor made by Sánṭáls

Paurá chuạ, grog shop

Páyá, lake, pool

Páyár idí, sway in one direction by wind

Peádá,[o] messenger, soldier, policeman

Peáj,[o] onion

Peláu: á, peláu enái, kedeái, force a passage

Peṇcho:ái, peṇch enái, kedeái, overcome, press down, narrow, make small

Penḍko, peṉrko:, peṉrolko:, unripe

Pepṇret, trumpet, flute

Peṛá, friend, relative

Peṛái eái, peṛá ená, kedeái, entertain friends, make friends

Peṛá pahánṛá, friends and relatives

Pere: á:, fulness, filled

Perej„o: á, pere: ená, kedeái, be filled, be full

Peṛsango: á, peṛsang ená, kedeái, glance off

Pese:, triangular

Peská, testicle

Peṭ dándiá, glutton

Peṭe: lipí, blasted grain

Peṭe peṭe, crowded, jammed together

Peṭerbáre,* a kind of tree

Peṭero: á, peṭer ená, kedái, twist

Phaạd, army, crowd [open

Phádá, unenclosed, exposed,

Phádá phudu, fluttering

Pailáo,° renowned, firmament, expanse

Phákuṇrá,? ear of corn

Phándái ái, phándá kedeái, kick as a horse

Phánk, vain, empty, dear

Pháph uḍáute, sneeringly, mockingly, ridiculingly, laughingly

Phárάko: á, phárak ená, kedeái, separate one's self

Phaṛchhá, clear (as the sky), evident, open

Pháṛí, a quarter of meat, shoulder

Phariạ:ái, phariạ enái, kedeái, recover from sickness, cure, become well [ness

Phariạ mone, pureminded-

Pharkáu:ái, pharkáu enái, kedeái, fly away

Phárśí, language, tongue (also *párṣi*) [noose

Phásí, deceit, difficulty, snare,

Phásí:ái, phásí enái, kedeái, hang, kill

Phásíḍáng, gallows

Phasiạrá ái, enái, kedái, deceive, defraud, inveigle

Phasiạrá, deceiver

Phashkáu: á, phashkáu enái, kedeái,? escape, let go, slip, away

Phás phus, conspiracy, plot

Phásuṛo: á, phásuṛ ená, kedeái, fruitless, in vain, slip away

Pháṭár pháṭáro: á, pháṭár ená, kedái, devour, gnaw, make a noise in eating

Pháṭoko:ái, pháṭok enái, kedeái,° shut up, confine

Pháṭok,° a prison

Phautí, useless, rejected, masterless, ownerless, neglected, lazy, idle, empty (house, &c.)

Pheder phedero:ái, pheder enái, complain, mutter, chatter in anger

Phedo: á, phe: ená, kedeái, fly back and hit (as boughs)

Phen, parable

Phen roṛ, speak in parables

Phente, enigmatically

Phenchoṛo: á, phenchoṛ ená, kedái, glance off, rebound

Phenkáu:ái, phenkáu eṉái, kedeái, conceal from justice, stray, wander, drive away, run away

Pheṉro:ái, pheṉr enái, kedeái,[o] foam, froth

Pheṭáṉr, heifer

Phepṛá:ái, phepṛái enái, act the hypocrite, simulate ignorance, stumble

Pheṛ, pheḍ, near, by side of, bottom, below

Pheṛ khon, from the beginning or bottom

Pheṛte, low, near the ground

Pheṛ re, in the neighbourhood

Pher enderái, three days after tomorrow

Pher sátom,? three years hence

Pher baipár,[o] trade of a money-lender, traffic

Pher ke pher, again, back again

Pheṛpáng,? sink in the mud, stick in the mud

Pher phár, changes

Phikir ái, kedái,[o] contrive, be cunning, deceive

Phink leka, very white

Phínphíniyá, very fine and white clothes

Phiráu: á, phiráu enái, kedeái,[o] restore, give back, alter, change, change colour

Phirí, shield

Phiṛipháng, cloudless

Phirkodo:ái, phirkot„ enái, kedeái, sullen, silent (of a woman)

Phirphiri,? jewel

Phirphiro:ái, phir enái, kedeái, be angry (of a woman) kick quickly (as a cow)

Phiṭkirí,† alum

Phográ, toothless

Phŏká: á, phokái ená, phoká kedeái, blister, fester

Phŏká, blister from burning

Phoko phoko, be very fat

Phohphoko:ái, phokoi enái, phoko kedái, foam

Phoktiá, wit, ridicule

Phŏphundá, musty, stale, dusty, dirty

Phormásái ái, phormás kedái,° bespeak

Phoṛo: á, phoṛ ená, kedái, burst forth (as water)

Phoro:? °crumble

Phorphundí, hypocrisy, fraud, artful, deceitful

Phoṭá: á, phoṭá ená, kedeái, be skinned (by a burn, blister, &c.), peel

Phudphudáu:ái, phudáu enái, kedeái, clap wings

Phuktí, phŏktiá, fun, mirth, quaintness

Phukut" phukut", dying, at the last gasp, rumbling in stomach

Phuláu:ái, phuláu enái, kedeái, be proud, distend

Phulí, strong liquor before water is added

Phúlí, mote, eyeball

Phúlpatáu, friendship, communion, concord; give gifts, mutually in token of friendship

Phundi,? make false excuses (see *phorphundi*)

Phuphuáu ái, ádeái, breathe hard, snort

Phuṛog ái, phuṛo: kedái, make cups of leaves

Phuṛog", cup of leaves

Phusláu eái, kedeái,° flatter, inveigle

Phusphus, phusphusrŏṛ, whisper

Phuṭ, melon; split, a sudden snap (of rope, &c.)

Phuṭáu: á, phuṭáu ená, kedái, break forth, be revealed (as secrets)

Pichhaurí, sheet, the large cloth worn in winter by men, but single

Piko poko:ái, pokoi enái, poko kedeái, be fat-cleeked, corpulent

Píla, spleen

Pilchu háṉrám, the first man

Pilchu buḍdhí, the first woman

Pindá, verandah

Pínḍá, altar

Pinká,? cigar

Pípá,† cask

Pipiriáng, butterfly

Pipní, eyeball, apple of eye

Píṛhí, generation

Piri,? snake basket

Piṛiáng piṛiáng ái, kedái, cry as a bird

Piṛiá piṛiá, just dying, at the last gasp

Piring,? misconduct

Piri: pirijo: á, piri: enái, kedái, ooze out, sun just appearing

Piríto: áling, pirít enái, kedeái,° long for, love, feel great affection for

Pisír, to open, distend, *pasír*

Piskij, part the grass in search of something

Pít,† gall; a sickness (like smallpox or itch)

Pítal,† brass

Piṭhạ, bread, loaf

Piṭí:, skein of hemp, a kind of girdle worn at sword dance

Piṭíjo:ái, piṭi: enái, kedái, coil up (as snake), be matted (as hair, &c.), wind up

Piṭuk,° glutton

Piyáng páyáng, dawn, just beginning to get light

*Pochá,** a kind of fish

Pochrá, cowardly

Podíná,† mint

Podná, string worn round the arm

Poḍo, fig tree

Podo:ái, pod enái, kededi, remove, have two places of residence, change villages

Pohá, plant

Pohá: á, pohá ená, bud (as a tree)

Poho, locust

Poi, result of an evil act, consequences, punishment

Pokpoko:ái, pokoi enái, poko kedái, puff out the cheeks, be fat (see also *phoko phoko*)

Pŏkrŏk,? ugly

Pokrot,,, corpulent, flabby, fat-cheeked

Polo: polo:, hardly visible, indistinct

Ponḍá:ái, ponḍ kedái, whiten

Ponḍ, white, clean

Pondá, rotten wood, wood hard on one side and soft on the other

Pon, four

Ponjángáwán, quadruped

Ponhonḍ, square, four-cornered, all round

Poṛ, low scrubby jungle

Poráiní, a white lily

Porho, result, fruit, confidence

Pormondá, tyranny, oppression

Pŏrŏb, festival, feast

Pŏrŏbo:ái, porob enái, kedái, to keep a festival

Poroi poroi dá:, showers

Poságo: á, posá: ená, kedái, fly open, break in pieces, snap break

Poská, soft, week (generally of wood or cotton)

Posṛá eái, kedeái, despise, scorn

Pŏstá, doe

Poṭá, stomach

Poṭágo: á, poṭá: ená, kedeái, peel bark from trees, peel off (the skin)

Potám, dove

Pŏtásír, large vein

Poṭáu ái, ená, kedái, smear, plaister with mud (see *paṭáu*)

Poṭiyá tárup, tiger

Poṭojo: á, poṭoi: ená, be sprained, out of joint

Poṭomo: á, poṭom enái, kedeái, wrap up

Poṭom mid,,, wrap up together, enclose

Poṭoro: á, poṭor ená, kedeái, cleanse, dress (a fowl, &c.), pluck feathers, dig up grass, steal clothes

Poṭrá, corpulent, large stomach (as in spleen)

Powá, a weight about one pound

Púchháu eái, kedeái,° ask into a house, invite, entertain, treat kindly

Puḍi,* a kind of fish

Puhí,? float of fishing-line

Pui pui ái, enái, kedeái, surfeit

Puj,? matter from a sore

Pujá aghá,° idolator

Pukrí,° tank

Pul,† bridge

Pungí, tobacco-pipe made of leaves

Pupulhet,,, hazy, pale moonlight

Púrab,† east

Purái,* a kind of vegetable or fruit, "paiság"

Puráu: á, puráu ená, kedeái,° fulfil, accomplish, full price, &c.

Purhút bábṛen, Brahmins

Púrí, world

Purkhạ,° old men, elders

Puruchhun, excellence, merit

Púrún,° complete, faultless, perfect, full

Pusí, cat

Pusindo: ái, pusind kedái,° please, choose, like, select

Pusrí, prickly heat

Pustak, puthí,† book

Pusṭáu ái, kedái, pronounce clearly, articulate

Puṭhujo: ái, puṭhui: enái, kedái, sprain, remove entrails, gut

Puṭi: ái, puṭi enái, kedeái, bloat, not to digest food

Putlạ, idol,? a piece of a cart

R

Rábáng, cold
Rábáng din, winter
Ráboṛ ái, enái, kedeái, scratch
Rách, part of weaver's apparatus
Ráchá ái, kedeái, go to stool
Ráchá, compound, garden
Ráchá te, outside (*i.e.*, the house)
Ráchágo: á, ráchá: enái, kedeái, break off, pluck off, pull out, pick off
Ráddahá, evil person, vile person
Rádrádáu, drag along ground, haul along ground (make the sound of "rad, rad"), crackle
Ráekákáṉrbá, chameleon
Rág ái, rá: kedeái, cry, whine, wail for dead, scream
Rárá: i:, crier
Rá: jarwá, call together
Rágumchá:, with coarse dishevelled hair; a kind of root
Rahám, salted, over-seasoned
Rahan, rohon, employment, trade, occupation, customary work
Raháu: á, raháu ená, kedái, sleep, as hand or foot
Raher, a kind of pea, "rahar"
Ráhí, steady,? peaceful,? mild,? *palki*
Rái,[o] a caste of this name
Rạí,[o] mustard
Ráibári:, angel,? arranger of marriages
Rái duhái,[o] supplication
Ráj,† zemindar, king, landlord, magistrate
Rájo:ái, ráj enái, kedeái,[o] be a king, reign
Ráj rapáj, sovereign, king, magistrates
Ráj disom,[o] country
Ráj dháni, palace
Ráji:ái, ráji enái, kedeái,[o] be pleased, consent, be willing
Rájá muni, a kind of bird
Ráján bháján, splendour, hospitable, magnificent (giving many *ghaṛas* of grog at a wedding)
Rákábo:ái, rákáp„ enái, kedeái, raise
Rakhni,? prohibition, embargo
Rámá, nails, claws
Rámpá ái, rámpái ená, rámpá kedeái, surround with thorns
Rán, rándá:, medicine
Rán, rán taká, bribe
Randákap,* a kind of fish

Ránákháp, notches to ascend by, kind of steps

Ránbŏrá,? "dál," a kind of pea, "biri"

Randí,† widow

Rángá chŏngá, knotted, gnarled, rough (as trees), thorny

Rangáini, a wide-spreading weed like a thistle

Rangáu:ái, rangáu enái, kedeái, be indignant

Ráni,† a queen

Ránre,? relent

Ráṇth,† rays of sun, light

Ránu, drug put into liquor to make it intoxicating, leaven

Rápáboṛ áling, enáling, tear with nails, mutually scratch (see *ráboṛ*)

Rápáchá: áling, fight, seize by hair mutually (see *ráchág*)

Rápág eái, rápá: enái, kedeái, burn the dead, cook, roast

Ráprápá: ái, ráprápá enái, kedeái, have disorderly hair, fence with thorns, sprawl on ground

Rápudo: á, ráput,, enái, kedeái, break, crack, crumble, pierce

Raṛ ái, kedái, sing sweetly, sound sweet

Ráṛái ái, ráṛá ená, kedeái, let go, loosen, opèn, free, release, unbind, untie

Ráṛo: á, ráṛ akáná, tumble, foam (as a river through rocks)

Raṣ, produce of the earth

Rásá,[o] juice, honey

Ráse, soup, juice of meat

Rásiá áling, enáling, kedáling, share together, have partneship

Rásiáte, together

Rásít,[o] receipt

Raskạ:ái, raskạ enái, kedái, desire

Raskạ, delight, desire, wish

Rassi áto, rassi bŏstí, large village, town, city

Rásun,[o] garlic.

Rátá kuṛí, girl past the age of marriage

Rátáng, frost, snow

Ráth,[o] car, rays of sun

Ráth gaḍí, chariot

Rau,? fly

Ráuráu:ái, ráuráu kedeái, make a noise, or row, crackle (as fire), scold

Ráwál, easy, light

Re, in, among, between, against

táláre, in the midst, among, between

Reáṛ, cold, cool

Reáṛo:ái, reáṛ enái, ke dingná, become cold, or numb

Rebedo: á, rebet„ kedái, crowd in, hide, tuck up, push in, squeeze in

Reben, consent

Rebeno:ái, reben enái, kedeái, agree, be willing, desire, like, consent, wish

Rechŏng, perhaps (in comp.)

Rehḍá, kind of earth of which cows are fond

Rehet„, root, foundation

Rehedo: á, rehet„ ená, kedái, take root

Rej ái, re: kedái, take by force, ravish, rob, seize, steal

Rere: á:, spoil, theft, stolen property

Rejimeng, chatterer, talkative (of women)

Relo: á, rel ená, kedái, winnow in a fan [hold

Remo: á, rem ená, kedeái, take

Reme:, part of intestines of a cow, paunch

Renge:, hungry, in want of, be desirous for, poor

Renge: lái:, hungry

Renge: rábáng, hungry and cold, abject, poor

Renge: ore:, abject, hungry

Renge: ákál, famine

Renkáu,? to have an appetite

Re̱nre, a kind of fish

Re̱nre gocho, the whisker-like protrusions of a "*re̱nre*"

Meráḍ, mischief, violence

Rese:,? crush, tread upon

Ret, file, rasp, sand

Ret„, small bundle of medicine *chun*, &c., a packet

Reṭhá reṭhí, enmity, ill-feeling, squabble, disagreement

Reṭhe, small, dwarfish

Reṭhe tárup, small kind of tiger

Ret rette, in line

Ret ret ále, enále, ket koái, put into line

Riáu: ále, riáu enále, kedále, consult, make up a story, come to a determination

Riáu rájoṭ, council, determination, plan, opinions

Ribi: ribi: edái, kedái, sprinkle, ooze out, drop

Ribŏng kŏbŏng, decrepit, aged, weak through sickness

Richí,* a bird of prey

Rído: á, rít„ ená, kedái, grind, pulverize [powder

Rít„ lemeng, grind to

Riḍedo:ái, riḍet,, enái, kedeái, be pinched, be caught, be hindered, be crushed by a weight, be squeezed, be jammed

Rigám chágám, noise of some one coming slowly along

Rigdáu: á, rigdáu ená, kedeái, drag, push, scrape along

Righí: á, righí enái, kedái, make a ring (in wood)

Righí, a ring made on wood either for ornament or as a stop

Rijháu:ái, rijháu enái, kedeái, sway, influence, have a bias, please

Rijo:ái, rij enái, kedeái,[o] desire

Rilá málá, clear, open, pure, spotless, innocent

Rimí kedeái, find a dead animal in the jungle (as a cow torn by tiger, &c.)

Rimí tingi:ái, tingi enái, exult, be merry, dance for joy

Rímílo: á, rímíl kedái, cloud

Rímíl, cloud

Rímíl sáḍe, thunder

Rín,[o] credit

Rín jom, borrow

Rín ṭaká, debt

Rín topá:, forgive debts

Ringáu:ái, ringáu enái, kedeái, soar, sing with high voice

Ripit,, eyelid

Ripipijo: áling, ripipi: enáling, wink, make signs with eyes mutually

Riṛh, ridge (of field), edge of something bevilled

Risá sím, hen with feathers standing forward

Rochodo:ái, rochot,, enái, kedeái, break (as head on a tree)

Rodo: ái, rot,, enái, kedeái, tie hair in a knot, arrange hair or whiskers

Roḍojo: á, roḍoi: ená, kedái, drop (as rain, &c.), wring out

Roḍgo, stony ground; a kind of fish

Rofhái eái, enái, kedeái,[o] be reconciled, be established in a place

Rog,, ái, ro: ená, kedái, punch, make holes, prick, sew, pierce, gore, goad, cut with chisel

Ro: mid,,, sew on, repair

Ro: eset,, sew up

Ro:bhugaḡ, pierce a hole

Rogá, disease, ulcers

Rog bighin, sickness

Rogi, sick, diseased

Rogoṛ, a stream

Rŏgŏṛte, steadily, uniformly, continually

Rohed eái, rohet,, kedái, quarrel, reproach, upbraid, reprove, abuse, scold (see also *ruhed*)

Rohoi: á, rohoi kedái, plant

Rohon, occupation (see *rahan*)

Rohoṛo: á, rohoṛ ená, kedeái, dry, wither

Rohoṛ khaṛangáu: á, khaṛangáu ená, dry up

Rohoṛ, dry, crisp, dried up

Roká, freshly made

Rokoi:, a small snail

Rŏkŏm,° sort

Rokoṛo:ái, rokoṛ kedeái, sleep on something rough so as to pain the body

Rol, an astringent fruit used in tanning "kasáphal"

Rol muiṇ, black ant

Rolo: á, rol ená, kedeái, take meat off the fire, fall or come out of fire

Romjhom,? anklet

Rongo: á, rongoi ená, rongo kedeái, burn up, singe, scorch, wither, singe the bristles of a pig, or feathers of a chicken

Rŏpdhŏp ái, hedeái, conceal a fault, connive

Ropo: ákin, ropo enákin, fight (as bulls) mutually stick, argue (see *rog,,*)

Ropoṛ áling, enáling, converse, fight (in words), argue, quarrel (see *roṛ*)

Ropoṛá: conversation, quarrel, argument

Roṛ, speech

Roṛ ái, ádeái, kedeái, speak, explain, relate, mention, talk

Roṛ jong, converse

Roṛ sahi, testify

Roṛ ruaṛ, answer

Roṛ sáḍe, preach, proclaim

Roṛ párom, provoke by speaking rudely

Roṛ sohod,,, advocate, plead another's cause

Roṛ lánd, life, walk, conversation, consummation of marriage

Roṛ suk, abuse, provoke

Roṛ midá:, determination, arranged plan

Ros,° juice

Rŏse rŏsete, gently, softly, slowly

Rŏsŏm rŏsŏm, indisposed, slightly unwell, gently, quietly,

Roṭe, frog, toad; to singe? heat?

Rúạ, disease, fever, sick, ill

Rúạ háso, sickness, pain

Rúaṛ, back, again (adverb)

Ruaṛo:ái, ruaṛ enái, hedeái, return, turn, bring back, change

Rúbo: á, rúp„ ená, kedeái, blow down, uproot by storm, knock down, push over

Rúchup„ rúchup„, crackling in eating something hard

Ruhed eái, ruhet„ kedeái, abuse, scold, quarrel, reproach, reprove, upbraid

Ru: hedi:, reviler, calumniator, accuser

Ruhi, "rui" a kind of fish

Rúi† cotton (of the country)

Rúkạ,° chisel

Rukhiạ:ái, rukhiạ ená, kedeái, be saved, be preserved, escape

Ruk rábon, scarcity, destitution

Ruku: á, rukui ená, ruku kedeái, shake, swing

Rumbui: chumbujo: ále, chumbui: enále, be festive, keep festival

Rumu:ái, rum enái, kedeái, shake the head (the custom in worshipping)

Rund runáu:ái, runáu enái, kedeái, shiver with cold

Rundá,* a wild cat

Rúpạ,† silver

S

Sabágo: á, sabá: ená, kedái, be tasteless, become insipid

Sabásí, greatness, glory, praise, renown

Sabási ái, enái, ocho kedeái, praise

Sábít,† excellent

Sábo: ái, sáp„ enái, kedeái, catch, arrest, discover

Sásápí:, catcher

Sábudo: á, sábut„ ená, kedeái,° give evidence, prove, settle

Sádá,† plain (adj.), pure, unmixed

Sáḍe, sound, voice, marriage portion

Sáḍe:ái, sáḍe enái, kedái, give a sound

Sáḍ, utter, speak loudly

Sadháu:ái, sadháu enái, het táiá, commit suicide

Sádom, horse

Sádom muíṇ, red ant

Sáe kedái, finish

Sáegát„, rough, uneven, not smooth

Saṅgát„ roṛ, speak irritatingly, vex

Safhạí ái, safhá ená kedeái,° clean, cleanse, purify, sanctify, give explanation

Ságá:, a kind of early grass

Ságáṛ, cart

Ságeno: á, ságen ená, kedái, bud, grow

Sagui: bagui:, disorderly conduct, confusion, uncertainty

Ságuno: á, ságun ená, ádeái, arrange marriages, be successful, lucky, arrange anything

Sáhạí ái, ái, ádeái, bless, praise, thank, help, assist, favour

Sáhán, fuel

Saháṛo: á, saháṛ ená, kedeái; sá: á, sá ená, kedeái, put aside, separate

Saháu: á, saháu ená, kedái,° bear, endure

Sáheb,† gentleman, sir

Sáhed ái, sáhet„ kedái, breathe

Sahí, true, proper

Sahí juhí: á, juhí ená, kedáling, correct, arrange, fix

Sáhobo: á, sáhop„ ená, kedái, hold, contain, fill in

Sahráj,* a kind of large bird

Sahtá,° cheap

Sái ái, ená, kedái, remove to another place (see *sá*)

Sạil, wild male buffalo

Saintáu, to arrange

Sáj,† ornament, dress

Sajai,° punishment

Sajáu:ái, sajáu enái, hedeái,° prepare, train

Sákám, leaf

Sakaráth, a feast occurring about the middle of January

Sákhí,† witness

Sákom, bracelet

Sákor,* a kind of tree, "*sij*"

Sakṛá, narrow

Sakṛí, crumbs, morsels

Saktí,° hardship, severity

Saktí:ái, saktí enái, kedeái, punish, take an oath

Sákwá, flute of horn

Salá ái, enái, kedeái, pick out

Sálágo:ái, sálá: enái, kedeái, mix, collect

Saláh,† counsel, advice

Salámí, offering, present to a great man

Sálás, rare, new, strange, novel

Sálás kathá, a discovery

Salá saláte, with

Salgáu: á, salgáu ená, kedái°, set fire, kindle, lighten

Sámá,* a kind of wild grass

Samá chákŏr,* a kind of large bird

Samágo: á, samá: enú, kedái, cut off, cut up meat

Sámáng, front

Sámángá:, offered (in sacrifice, &c.)

Sámángo: á, sámáng ená, kedeái, offer up sacrifice, present before

Sámángre, before, in front, in presence of, in opinion of

Sámáng se:, sámáng ren or *reá*, opposite

Sámáng daṭṭá, front teeth

Sámánom, gold, golden, a jewel

Sámbáu:ái, sámbáu enái, kedái, fill up (or in), place in, hold, contain

Sámbiro:ái, sámbir enái, kedeái, sleep on the back, throw on to the back

Samboṛáu: á, samboṛáu ená, kedeái, sustain, support, contain, assist, hold up, be firm

Sámge:ái, sámge enái, kedeái, be accustomed to, get friendly with (after a short time)

Samkhol, a kind of bird, a kind of fish, "gendalia"

Sámṭáu: á, sámṭáu ená, kedái, roll up clothes, &c., tuck up, fold up, collect together, prepare, make ready

Sán, grinding-stone, or wheel; a caste of blacksmiths

Saná edeá, kedeá, wish, desire

Sanám, all

Sanám lekáná, every kind

Sanám hilo:, always, eternally

Sanám ṭhen, everywhere

Sanámá:, entireness, completeness

Sánch,[0] mould, frame

Sánḍ, bull

Sánḍáng, sleepy fellow (used in anger)

Sanḍásí,† tongs, pincers

Sandes, present to children, relatives, &c., offerings

Sándi, cock

Sangá, beam, rafter

Sángárhe:ái, sángárhe enái, kedeái, prop up, assist (a sick person), lean against, support

Sánge: áko, sánge enáko, ket koái, crowd, assemble

Sánge idí, increase (*e.g.* village, company, &c.)

Sánge hoṛ, a crowd

Sanghái eúi, sanghá enái, kedeái, marry second time, marry a widow or deceased brother's wife

Sangíng, distance, distant

Sáṇhái, to investigate

Sánk, goose

Sáṉrgom, oppression

Sántáu eái, kedeái,[o] persecute, oppress

Sásántáui:, oppressor

Sáṇw, company

Sáṇw hoṛ, sáṇwten, comrade, companion

Sáṇwte, with, together with

Sáṇwái ái, ená, kedái, grow in abundance, have good crops, rain sufficiently

Sáṇwái, abundance, years of plenty (particularly of rain)

Saṇwár, level, even

Saṇwáro:ái, enái,[o] amend, reform

Sáṇwráu:ái, saṇwráu enái, kedeái, amend, reform, bring back, be reconciled

Saṇwhá: á, saṇwhái enái, kedeái, support (so as to prevent falling), repair

Saṇwrá, grey

Sápáp, give mutual evidence against; effects, furniture

Sápáp ále, enále, join hands (see *sáb*)

Sáp, ṭhaharáu, support (*e.g.* catch hold of a falling person or thing)

Sápṛáu:ái sápṛáu ená, kedeái, make (or get, or be) ready, prepare

Sár, arrow, reed from which arrows are made

Saṛ, saddle of an elephant

Sárá,[o] funeral pyle

Sárám, sárámpárá, elk

Saráp áiái, ádeái,[o] curse

Sárápen, accursed

Sarbharáu, move, excite

Sárdi, very

Sárdi sengel, conflagration

Sárdi setong, great glare

Sáre: á:, remaining, remainder, rest, remnant

Sárejo: á, sáre: ená, kedeái, reserve food for another, leave something (after eating)

Sárháu:ái, sárháu enái, kedeái, praise

Sárháu leká, praiseworthy, commendable

Sáṛhe: á, sáṛhe ená, kedái, bud

Sáṛhe:, vigorous, strong, (usually of plants)

Sáṛhe: hoṛmo, robust, good health

Sarí: á, sarí ená, kedái,† prove, ascertain, believe

Sarí, true

Saríge, truly

Sarí ochoi, to prove

Saríá:, truth

Sariáu: á, sariáu ená, kedeái, arrange, put in order, dress a fowl, &c.

Sarím, thatched roof, thatch

Sárjom, a kind of tree, "sál"

Sarkár, teacher, master

Sárlágo:ái, sárlá: enái, kedeái, be pierced with a thorn or splint

Sáro: á, sár ená, kedái, expand, blow (as flowers), open out hood (as cobra)

Sáron,? play tricks

Sárreṛo: á, sárreṛ enái, kedeái, to be full to overflowing, be brimfull

Sárságun,° deliberation before some great event, consultation, marriage arrangements, success, good results

Saṛsaṛáu:, be anxious

Sársárjom, a kind of "sál" tree

Sasamṭáui:, a reaper, collector

Sásáng,° turmeric "baldi"

Sasantáui:,° persecutor

Sáset,,, toil, trouble, pain

Sásedo:ái, sáset,, *enái, kedeái*, distress, vex, punish

Sastá,† cheap

Satálá:, for, through, on account

Sátáu,? open

Sáte, eave of a house

Saṭo: á, saṭ enái, kedái, be forward, fashioned, ready

Sáṭob, get a knock on chin so as to bite the tongue between the teeth

Sátom, the year after

Sáṭ páṭ, sáṭmente, quickly

Satrú,† enemy

Sattam, breast, dug, nipple, udder, teat

Sáttáte, by means of

Sáu,° merchant, creditor

Sauṛí, thatch, a grass used for thatching

Sau sau lo, burn brightly

Sauthí mirich,? pepper

Se, or

Se bángá, (yes) or no

Se:, side, towards

Sejo: á, se: enái, kedeái, incline, lean to one side, turn towards, direct towards

Seá: á, seá ená, kedeái, rot, decay, corrupt; metaph; conceal, keep hidden

Sebíl, taste, sweet taste

Sedái, ancient

Sedái re, anciently

Sedái soro, traditions

Seke: seke, tinkling

Sekhí sekhí, angry

Sekre:, a kind of berry

Seledo: á, selet,, enái, kedeái, to mix, unite

Selet,,, with

*Selimbo bahá,** a kind of yellow flower

*Selip sámáng bahá,** a kind of red flower

Sendrá, hunt, sport

Sendrá seno:, go to hunt

Sendrá kárká, a hunt

Sengel, fire, to set on fire

Sengel dá:, the Sántál idea of the great flood

Sengel ere, a kind of woodpecker

Sengel mármár, centipede ("Kángochar," yellow and black, poisonous)

Sengel tetí, Guinea hen

Seno: ái, sen enái, go, walk, obey, act upon, practice

Seno: heju: i:, a passer-by, traveller

Seṇ seṇ sáhet,? senktoṛ, pant, be out of breath

Sente,? direction of the compass

Sepingno: á, sepingn ená, kedeái, hold open in hand, put hand under (something to support it), hold, catch, support from beneath

Ser,† about two pounds

Serále, duck (wild)

Seredo: á, seret,, ená, kedeái, crush

Serengn ái, kedái, sing

Seserengi:, singer

Sereng, song

Seṛeṛ seṛeṛ, nauseous

Sere sere: á, sere ená, kedái, discharge matter

Sermá, sky, heaven, year

Sermá ráj, kingdom of heaven

Sermáren ráibári, spiritual messenger, angel

Serom, neck of animal, back of neck

Sesá:, final, conclusion, end

Sesre, at length, finally

Setá, dog

Setá lekán hoṛ, a vile person

Setá:, morning

Setegn, a spring

Setengno: á, setengn ená, kedái, ooze out

Seṭero: á, seṭer enái, kedeái, arrive, reach, deliver, convey

Setong, glare, sunshine

Setongo: á, setong ená, kedái, be hot

Setop, to nourish

Sevok ái, ádeái,° worship

Serná ái, kedeái,[O] worship, serve
Shŏrŏm,[O] shame [fect
Siddh,[O] pay of a teacher,? per-
Sidhi, collect rent
Sido: á, sít,, ená, kedái, pick off the leaves
Sih, louse
Sika, the Sántál spots made by fire on left arm in youth
Sikạriyá,[O] hunter, sportsman
Si: káṭup, little finger
Sikháu eái, kedeái,[O] teach
  Siknat,,,[O] teaching, doctrine
Sikhláu eái, kedeái, chasten
Siki: siki:, passionate (used of women)
Siknrit,,, mosquito [net
  Siknrit,, jhálí, mosquito
Síko:ái, sík enái, kedeái, be like, resemble, copy
Sikṛí:ái, sikṛí enái, kedeái,[O] chain
  Sikṛí,[O] chain
Sikyom bahá,[*] a kind of large white flower
Silí, hair rope
Silping, door
  Silping sing, close the door
Silung piṭung, filthy, dirty
Sím, cock, fowl, hen
  Sím rág,,, to crow
  Sím hopon, chicken
Símạ,[O] border, limit
Sing, day
  Sing sáṭup, all day, continually
  Sing mársál, daylight
  Sing lái gnindá lái, all day and night
Sing,? lion
Sing áṛá, a vegetable. "kandol ság"
Singár payár, evening
Singno: á, sing ená, kedeái, shut, shut up, confine
Sinhásan,† throne
Sinit,,, privacy, private occasion or opportunity, lonely place
Sipạhi,[O] messenger
Sípi: á, sípi ená, kedeái, mix earth, or mortar, mix up one's rice and *dal* or vegetables in eating, pinch, take a handful
Sír, vein
Sirát,, bárát,,, very good meat
Sírhi: á, sírhi ená, kedái, prepare roof for thatch, spread thick boughs on the beams of a house
Siṛi:, smell (as bad fish or meat) stink
Siri ái, kedeái, seek for, look out for

Siri áni:, fortunate, lucky

Sirjáu: á, sirjáu ená, kedeái,[o] create, arise, be produced

Sirom, coarse grass used for baskets, &c.

Siropá, present, gift

Sirpui: bhagwá, very small *dhoti* (*nangoti*)

Sirri: birri:,* a tree with very small leaves

Sirubo: á, sirup,, enái, kedeái, suck in. [The Sántál mothers fill their new-born babies' ears with water and then suck it in]

Sísá,† lead, metal

Sísír dá:, dew

Sitet,,, beeswax

Sitká, pains of childbirth

Sitpasáre,? disorderly

Síy ái, si ená, kedái, plough

Si lahudo: á, lahut,, ená, kedái, plough and harrow, plough and prepare land (*i.e.* take out grass, &c.)

Siyáno: á, siyán enái, kedeái,[o] grow up, arrive at maturity, be cunning, crafty, be well grown

So: á, soi ená, so kedái, pound rice, carry a plough from field to field, scent, smell

So: rasá, incense, perfume

So: sunum, sweet-smelling oil

Sobod, wash clothes

Sŏbŏgo: á, sobo: enái, kedeái, pound, pierce, thrust through, prick, beat

Sodo:, a ditch, a small *nálá*, a stream

Sodoro: á, sodor ená, kedeái, represent, reveal, make a declaration, become public, advertise, proclaim

Sodor re, publicly

Sogág ái, sogá: kedeái, snap, peck (as birds), dart upon, strike (as snake)

Soghor, pretty

Sohág,? love

Sohor, red border of cloth, a city

Sohoro: á, sohor enái, kedeái, drag along (or down), push along (or down), make a border to a cloth, brush along before

Soi ái, enái, kedeái, extract, take out (*e.g.* thorns, &c.)

Sojhe eái, enái, kedeái, make straight, reform; straightforward, direct

Sŏkŏjo: á, sokoi: enái, kedeái, rinse, shake well (in hand), heave, shake from side to side (as water)

Sokto: á, soktoi ená, sokto kedeái,° strengthen, make firm, strong

Solho:ái, solhoi enái, solho kedeái,° be reconciled

Solok, peace, quiet, happiness

Sŏlŏngo: á, solong ená, kedeái, fill up, place in, be contained in

Sombát„,† good news, welfare, good tidings

Sombodo:ái, sombot„ enái, kedeái, fall, stumble, fall on face

Sombolo:ái, sombol enái, kedái, prepare for journey (*i.e.* cook food, get vessels together)

Somboṛáu:ái, somboṛáu enái, kedeái,° bear, support, endure (see also *sámbaṛáu*)

Sompáu:ái, sompáu enái, kedeái,° deliver up or over, entrust

Soná,† gold

Soná ágnui, gild

Soná chitą, leopard

Sonḍá, large side-teeth (of a tiger, boar, &c.), tusks, fangs (of a snake)

Sondṛe:ái, sondṛe enái, kedeái, push through a crowd, elbow one's way, pant

Sŏndro, scab of a sore

Sone sud, true

Songe, accompany, with

Songet ení:; companion

Songo: á, song ená, kedái, measure, a measure

Sonhár, goldsmith

Soṇko:ái, soṇk enái, kedeái, pant, be out of breath, tired

Sontoro:ái, sontor enái, kedeái, take care, be cautious, be on one's guard

Soṇwáring, grasshopper, cricket

Sopo, arm above the elbow

Soṛhá, a (round and hollow) plate of leaves

Sŏṛhái ái, soṛhá ená, ádeái, sew plate of leaves

Sor, near

Soro: á, sor enái, kedeái, be or bring near, come to

Sorsor hoṛ, sorren hoṛ, neighbour

Sor dingi, lately

Soro á, ená, kedeái, ordain (laws, &c.), appoint (customs, &c.), arrange, resolve, decree; determination, resolution

Soṛom, tasty, delicious

Sŏrŏnjám,° furniture &c. necessary for sacrifice, offerings

Soros, better, superior, more

Soroso:á, soros enái, kedeái, conquer, defeat, prevail, excel

Soṛtái eái, soṛtá enái, kedeái, sleep on side

*Soso** a kind of tree, "bhelwá"

Sŏsrŏi, grasshopper,? moth

Sotá,° fountain

Sotog eái, soto: kedeái, take care of a road, defend; brother next in age

Sŏtŏyá:, vulva fæmmeá

Sotrá:, have the menses

Subho,? a sore [abstinent

Subud,† temperate, moderate,

Suḅuṭ„ suḅuṭ„, companies, knots of people

Súd,† interest of money

Súde múle,° principal and interest

Súd águi, take interest

Suḍuro: á, suḍur ená, kedái, spout, flow, bleed, push, fall (as water)

Sugum sugum, in the dark, steal along at night

Suhánṛá ái, kedái, adorn, be populous

Suhíá:,° right, corrected, established, proved

Suhu:ái, suhui ená, suhu kedái, appropriate to self the good deeds of others, boast falsely

Súí,† needle

Sui á, sui ená, spring up (as seeds)

Sukái,? °dry, squeeze out

Sukh,† pleasure, pleasing

Sukhte, happily

Sukhá, prophet (Sántál)

Sukrí, hog, pig

Sului:, matter in a sore

Sulúk, peace, friendship, concord

Sulúko: áko, sulúk enáko, be reconciled

Sulúk idi, make up a quarrel

Suṃbaṛáu eái, kedeái,° endure, remain firm (see *sámbaṛáu*)

Sumjháu: á, sumjháu, kedái, give back, give up, (land, a pledge, &c.), devote, surrender, forfeit

Sumung, all round, completely, entirely, finished

Sumungo: á, sumung ená, kedeái, finish, complete

Sunḍ,† trunk, snout, epiglottis

Sunḍí gaddí, liquor-shop, drinking house

Sungá, sting

Sungá tejo, a kind of worm that stings

Sunrukui:, willow, water-plant

Sunum, oil

Sunum piṭhá, oilcake

Sunum len, express oil

Sunum muiṇ, black ant

Sunum bing, two-headed snake

Sunum gár, a kind of tree

Supṭáu: á, supṭáu ená, kedái, turn out well, be prosperous, be plentiful

Supoṭo: á, supoṭ ená, kedái, cook well, impart or have a pleasant taste, support a child in walking

Suptí, top or end of foot, small fan to clean rice

Súr,° greedy

Surogojá,* oil-plant

Suṛui: hor, narrow or difficult path

Surui: surujo:ái, surui: kedái, snuffle, sob

Suṛujo:, skulk

Súsí, an occasion against, cause of fault, ground of complaint

Susulúki:, kind, peaceable, peacemaker

Susúrbáng, wasp

Sutám, thread, cotton, wire, strings of musical instrument

Sut„ bahá:ái, bahá enái, kedeái, weave garland of flowers

Sut„ dá:, hole made in sand near river in order to filter the water

T

Tábero:ái, táber enái, kedeái,° do homage, fall prostrate, humbly salute, make obeisance

Ṭáben, pounded rice (*churá*)

Ṭábo: á, táp„enái, kedeái, pass through

Táhen ái, táheṇ enái, continue, remain, dwell

Táheno: á, dwelling

Táher, cucumber

Táháu:ái, kedái, fathom

Táharáu: á, ṭáharáu ená, kedeái, stick fast, be caught, entangled, stop, impede

Ṭáini, staff tipped with iron

Ták leká, upright, erect, motionless (applied to a man standing still)

Tákíjo: á, táki: ená, kedeái, run against, receive a concussion (on upper part of body), stumble, be offended

Táki:, dárám oppose

Ṭáká,† rupee

Ṭáká siropá, present of rupees

Tákoi ái, kedái, spin, wind

Tálá, half, middle

Tálá erá, middle wife, (there having been one before and one after)

Tálá gnindá, midnight

Tálámáláre, táláre, amid, among, in the middle, between

Tálá oṛág eái, oṛá: enái, kedeái, admit into house

Tálá ṭánḍí:ái, ṭánḍi ená, kedeái, be astonished, perplexed, in despair, in doubt

Ṭáláu: á, ṭáláu ená, kedeái, spend, pass, support, live

Tále,° palm tree

Tálebár, rich

Tálík ái, kedeái, take care of, provide for

Tálímo:ái, tálim enái, kedeái,° be instructed

Tálká,° palm of hand, sole of foot

Tálomo: á, tálom enái, kedeái, overflow, flow away

Tálsá, skin disease (in which spots appear over the whole body and disappear in a few minutes), rubbish,? parched bread made of flour

Tamassuk,† bond

Támbá,† copper

Támbháu:ái, támbháu enái, kedeái, restrain, hold, be prosperous in life, be successful, get over trouble, recover from sickness

Tambú,† tent

Ṭamḍáu:ái, ṭamḍáu kedái, search for, feel for, walk about?

Ṭamḍáu báṛái, grope about in dark

Támil,° authority, possession

Tamtá se:, scattered everywhere

Tán, kind of wolf

Ṭán, ṭánok, famine, scarcity, want of water

Ṭánáu: á, ṭánáu enái, kedeái,° draw

Ṭánḍái ái, ṭánḍá kedái, straddle, keep the legs wide apart

Ṭánḍi á:, cleared land, a plain

Ṭánḍi: á, ṭánḍi ená, kedeái, clear land of jungle, cleanse (a road, a room)

Ṭánḍí jong, go to stool

Ṭángá, axe

Tángingn ái, tángí kedeái, wait for, remain

Tapágo:, jerk something into the mouth

Tápám ále, enále, fight, battle

Tápingyo:ái, táping enái, ket táiá, beat the head in sorrow

Tápis, bold, brave, angrily, fiercely, powerfully

Tápse:, violent, jumping about, violently tossed up

Tárá, tárágе, half (see *tálá*)

Tarak mente, quickly

Táṛám ái, kedái, walk

Táṛám, a step

Táṛám chikná, footsteps, footprints

Táṛám lánḍhu, path made by walking

Taṛámre, on foot

Táṛán ái, enái, crouch, lie down in ambush

Táṛáng tiṛing, impatient, fiery, impetuous, harsh

Ṭáṛáng ṭuṛung, tinkling sound of pots, &c., when struck to test if they are sound

Tárásing / *máráng tárásing*, } about four o'clock

huḍing tárásing, about six o'clock

Ṭáráu: á, ṭáráu ená, kedeái, pile up, sweep up or together, brush along (with hand)

Táren, shoulder

Táṛi,† juice, especially of palm tree

Tárko: á, tárkoi ená, tárko kedeái, jolt, shake up

Táru,° roof of mouth

Táru lándup, noseless, flat-nosed

Tárup, leopard

Tarwáṛí,° sword

Táse: á, táse ená, kedeái, dry, be spread out, expand

Ṭáṭ,† sackcloth

Tátáu:ái, tátáu enái, kedeái, be warned, be on one's guard

Ṭáṭáu: á, ṭáṭáu ená, kedái, be very crisp and dry, *i.e. dhán* which breaks to pieces in cleaning it

Ṭáṭṭí,† a kind of screen

Ṭaṭkámar, sudden, momentary

Tathá enái, he was struck by sudden fear or surprise

Tawágo: á, tawá: enái, kedeái, dash down

Táyám, crocodile

Táyo, clapping of hands

Táyoi ái, ená, kedeái, clap hands

Táyom mánrang, before,? behind

Táyomo: á, táyom ená, kedeái, be behind

Táyomte, behind, after

Táyomse:, backwards

Te: á, te ená, kedái, clean grain, winnow (the grain by letting it fall to the ground and moving the fan)

Teáro: á, teár enái, kedeái,[o] prepare, make or get ready

*Tegnáng,** brother-in-law, eldest sister's husband

Ṭehár,? be on trial

Teheng, to-day

Teheng gapá, these times, now-a-days

Teingno: á, teing ená, kedái, weave cloth

Tejo, caterpillar

Teke: á, teke ená, kedái, cook

Teke: teke:, jingling or grinding noise

Tekráu eái, kedeái, earnestly ask, earnestly enquire

Tele: á, tele ená, kedái, gather rice under the *dhenki*

Tele, louse

Tel náhán, tel khar, a funeral feast ten days after a relative's death

Telsaṇwár, brown, a light-coloured man

Ṭeme: dá:, shallow water

Ṭená, cage, stand for birds

Ṭenḍáro: á, ṭenḍár enái, kedeái, lean, rest one thing against another, rest on

Ṭenḍár máchi, chair with back, arm-chair

Tengen eái, kedeái, bring religious offerings, worship (demons), drive a nail through the cock's head (at funerals)

Ṭengoi:, small axe (*kulhári*)

Teṇgun ái, tiṇgu eái, tiṇgu enái, kedeái, stand, be security for, go bail, settle price, fix, be firm

Tengo thiro:, be calm

Tenjlo:ái, tenjlo enái, kedái, stretch one's legs after having kept them bent for some time

Teno: á, ten enái, kedeái, fasten down, press down, squeeze

Tenrejhá:, corpulent,? fat,? swelled out as dead man

*Tepai,** a kind of tree

Tepedo:á, tepet,, ená, kedeái, stop up, close up, fill up, block up, shut in

Tepeno: á, tepen enái, kedái, cross, put in tiers

Teráng, ái, kedái, shoot (with a bow)

Terdej ái, terde: kedái, shine (used of the moon)

*Terel,** a kind of tree, "kendu"

Tere tese, abundant (as flowers thickly strewn under a tree)

Ṭeṛhá,† crooked

Terom, bee

Terom rasá, honey

Ṭesá, prop

Tesnek, unchangeable

Tetáng, thirst

Tetángo:ái, tetáng kedeái, thirst

Ṭewáno: á, ṭewán ená, kedeái, recover, find (what the person is searching for), hear news of, determine, ascertain

Teweingno: á, teweing ená, kedeái, suspend, hold in one's hand, hanging

Ṭhag,† extortioner, cheat, swindler

Ṭhághen, prop

Ṭhái ṭhui, noise (of fighting, gun, &c.), slap

Ṭhák, marvellous, wonderful

Thákáu:ái, thákáu enái, kedeái,° be weary

Ṭhákedo: á, ṭháket„ ená, kedeái, impede, stop, arrest the course of

Ṭháket„ dohoi, detain, delay

Tháktháḱ, suitable

Ṭhák ṭhákáu:ái, ṭhákáu enái, shiver from cold, be liberal

Thák thákáu:, be anxious, solicitous

Thalí: á, thalí ená, kedeái, stick fast, sink into mud

Thángál thungulo:ái, thungul enái, kedeái, waddle, be infirm (from age, sickness, &c.), be disquieted

Ṭhángkáṭhŏṛáng, fluently; the noise made in throwing something down (as bamboos, &c.)

Ṭháṇw eái, enái, kedeái,† place, establish, marry, make room for

Thapái eái, thapá ená, kedeái,° beat, slap, beat off dust, &c.

Thár bhasáu:ái, thárbhasáu enái, kedeái, do quickly, naturally, unpremeditatedly, be astonished

Thárí,° plate (of brass)

Thár ke thár, in rows, in tiers

Thártháráu:ái, thártháráu enái, kedeái,° tremble, shiver as in ague

Ṭhasakáu: á, ṭhasak ená, kedeái, remove, move, stir, put in motion

Ṭháṭáṛ, haggard

Ṭhathinrá, leg below the knee

Ṭhá: ṭhog ái, ṭhá: ṭho: kedái, strike (wood, door, &c.), strike each other

Ṭhauká, all sorts, all kinds (of things) collection

Thaurá, collection of men

Thawágo:, dash down (see *tawágo:*)

Thawí, lodge, stay, stop

Tháyái eái, tháyá kedeái, kick

Ṭhebo: á, ṭhep. ená, kedeái, snap the fingers, fillip

Thekáu,? begin

Ṭhekáu:ái, ṭhekáu enái, kedeái, employ labourers, put fuel on fire

Ṭhekomo: á, ṭhekom ená, kedái, stick, adhere

Ṭhelá:ái, ṭhelá enái, kedái, become callous

Ṭheláu: á, ṭheláu éná, kedeái,° push, shove, haul, wrestle

Ṭhemá: á, ṭhemái ená, ṭhemá kedái, gird on, put on the waist (sword-belt, &c.)

Ṭhen, ṭhe:, by, near (prepos.)

Ṭhenre, near (adv.)

Ṭhen khon, from

Ṭhengá, staff, stick

Ṭhero:ái, ṭher enái, be bold, forward, bad-tempered (of children), thunder out

Ṭheṛeṭhepe, continually moving, wagging (as dog's tail, elephant's snout)

Ṭheṭhámuṇ, cross, peevish, contradictory, stubborn, obstinate, sneer, ridicule, cheat

Thetre, be tired?

Ṭhík,† just, right, correct, confirmed

Ṭhíká ái, ádeái,† let on contract or for hire

Ṭhikáná,† appointed place or distance, direction

Ṭhikán eái, enái, kedeái, appoint, appraise, value

Ṭhikiṛi,? dwarf woman, short woman

Ṭhilí, earthen pot or jug

Thir hatáṛ, adjourn

Thiro:ái, thir enái, kedeái, hush, wait, avoid, abstain, be quiet, silent, cease

Tho áiái, tho kedái, spit, expectorate

Thoblá, bunch (of keys, &c.)

Ṭhok,° a cheat (and *ṭhag*)

Thomborot,,, corpulent, fat, squat

Ṭhongá, a bit of bamboo used for holding oil

Ṭhongá sár, a quiver, a kind of small arrow

Thonká, thorphán, a line or band of men

Ṭhonoko:ái, ṭhonok enái, kedeái, adorn self, be handsome, dress finely

Ṭhop, a drop

Ṭhop ṭhop, drop-by-drop

Thopá (thope, thopi), bunch, tassel, cluster of fruit, &c.

Thoṛá,† a little

Thoṛá thoṛí, more or less

Thoṛá din khán, soon

Thŏrbŏk,? suds, froth

Ṭhoṛeng jáng, shin-bone

Thotiyá,⁰ slow of speech

Thoṭrá,⁰ stammering, stuttering, lisping

Thu: á, thui ená, thu hedeái, break (as vessel, egg, &c.), smash

Ṭhugo:ái, ṭhu: enái, kedái, hit the head against something (also applied to pots)

Ṭhui eái, ṭhui enái, ṭhu kedeái, aim at, sound (as a gun), hit mark

Ti, hand, wrist, arm

Ti jángá, hands and feet, limbs

Tiágo:ái, tiá: enái, kedeái, shoot (with a bow), bend bow, lead by hand, reach

Tiạro:ái, tiạr enái, kedeái, stretch one's self, stretch out hand

Ṭihá ṭáhe:ái, ṭáhe enái, kedeái, walk slowly from a sore leg, &c.

Ṭihạdo:ái, ṭihạt„ enái, kedeái, be dependent, be supported by, derive living from (used often of a widow)

Tíj,⁰ a thing

Tíj básut,⁰ property

Tík, tick

Ṭíkạ:ái, ṭikạ enái, kedeái,⁰ spot, tattoo, vaccinate; a spot, stain, the Sántál marks on the left arm

Ṭikáu:ái, ṭikáu enái, kedeái, stop, remain, stay

Tikikhá, be troubled, forsake work through bother, be bothered,• choose, have authority

Tikin ber, tikin ṭhík,⁰ noon

Tikin lon̲rá, tikin erá:, about one o'clock

Ṭikur, dry land, high land

Tilá,* a kind of tree

Ṭilhạ, island

Tilming, sesamen, oil-plant, "*til*"

Tín, tinạ:, how much, how many

Tín hábí:, how long, how far

Tín re, when, what time

Tín tirit„„, how large

Tín bongá, tín chándo, how many months

Tín mahán̩, tin sermá, how many days, how many years

Tín ud̩í, what little

Ting eái, kedeái, knock down (with a stone) to stone

Tingi ái, kedái, put wood on fire

Tingido:ái, tingit,, enái, kedeái, fall down senseless or suddenly, ring (as ears)

Tingná:ái, tingná kedái, weave (cloth)

Tiog ái, tio: ená, kedái, arrive, overtake

Tipiogo: áling, tipio: enáling, walk hand-in-hand

Tírejuge, eternity, for ever, eternal

T̩irhol ái, kedái, rub ears of corn grain in hand to get out the

Tiriáu: áko, tiriáu enáko, ket koái, stretch, be scattered

Tirio, fife, flute

Tiris,° thirty

Tiriskál, indefinitely long period, ever so long

Tirit,,, large, great

Tirmiráu:ái, tirmiráu enái, kedeái, flutter, toss about in agonies of death

Tir̩ong, a swallow

Tirubo:ái, tirup,, enái, kedeái, lean on or forward, stoop, bow the head, erect (house, &c.)

Tís, when, whenever

Tíshon̩, ever, whenever

Tíshon̩báng, never

Titáu,? be exhausted, faint, become weak

*T̩it̩i hisir bahá,** a kind of red wild flower

Titit,,, much, many

Titmál,? pledge, security

Titrí, virgins who at a marriage rub *haldi* on the bridegroom

*Titrin̩rhí,** a kind of bird. "*t̩ent̩eá*"

Tŏbág ái, tobá: kedái, peck (as a bird)

Todo:ái, tot,, enái, kedeái, dig up, root, pick out, pull off clothes, &c., take out

T̩od̩or, ring on wrist

Togoi: dat̩t̩ái ái, dat̩t̩á enái, kedái, grin, grind the teeth, gnash

Tohináto:ái, tohinát enái, kedeái, make or get ready, prepare

Tohob ái, tohop,, kedái, take a handful (*i.e.*, as much as is grasped between forefinger and thumb in reaping)

Tohodo:ái, tohot,, enái, stumble, get a blow (on feet or legs)

Tok, cudgel, pestle

Tok leká, erect

Ṭokáu:ái, ṭokáu enái, kedeái, admonish warn

Toke,? eat fast, stop up mouth of vessel with hand

Ṭoke:, a kind of lump on the eyelid, a stye·

Ṭohlá:, small jug

Tolo: á, tol ená, kedeái, bind, tie

Tol láṭijo:, bind the hands behind the back

Tol urij, bind up

Tol idí, carry captive

Tol samṭáu, fasten together, bind together

Tol oṛá:, prison

Ṭolá,† division of a village

Ṭolá áṛerenko, neighbours

Tolgoiám, wool, fur, hairy

Tolmojo: á, tolmoi: enái, kedái, dry up, wither, fade

Tolmojo: á, tolmoi: enái, kedái, dry up, wither, fade

Ṭŏlṭŏláu: á, ṭoláu ená, kedeái, quiver on water, dance about, rock

Ṭonḍáng, dried up, waterless

Tondári, umpire, judge, take care of

Tondári: á, tondári ená, kedái, to judge, settle disputes, &c., investigate (a case)

Ṭonge: á, ṭonge ená, kedeái, join together, knot, join the clothes of a young pair at marriage, splice, bind with iron

Ṭonge, joint

Tonko:ái, tonkoi enái, tonko kedeái, be refreshed, grow warm again, recover, pull up

Tonol, bond, fastening

Topá, to bury (the dead), wear much clothes, be abundant (as grass)

Topá, a grave

Topá marṃáu, dead and buried, be extinguished

Topágo: á, topá: ená, kedeái break

Topáṛ, cover

Topo:ái, topoi enái, topo kedeái, bathe, wet, steep, dip into, soak

*Topot,,,** an insect

Topot,,, topot,, sánḍi, cockfight

Toprámo: á, toprám ená, kedeái, rub with mud

Toṛ, squirrel, hook on end of scorpion's tail

Toṛ eái, kedeái, sting (as a bee)

Ṭoráu: á, ṭoráu ená, kedeái, finish, end

Tormoyo,? sit carelessly

Toroḍáng, fish-basket

Toroi:, ashes

Torojo: á, toroi: ená, kedeái, burn up, dry up, reduce to ashes

Ṭoṭhá, pergunnah, part, side

Totká, nape of neck

Ṭoṭko, bells (for cows, &c.)

*Ṭoṭo,** wild cat [wild

Totoro, uncouth, uneducated,

Totṛá, stammerer

Towá, milk

Towá daká, rice and milk, "*khír*"

Towá nuṇnuhi:, a suckling

Towá dáre, mother (tree of milk)

Ṭoyá, jay

Toyo: á, toi ená, kedái, to be topsided, spring up (as one end of a piece of wood, or of a cart)

Toyu, jackal, fox

Ṭuạr, orphan

Ṭuạr amár, orphan and friendless

Túbedo:ái, tubet,, enái, kedeái, fill up a hole (spoken sometimes of a guest metephorically), stop the ears

Ṭúí, peak of roof, top, end, summit

Tuing goje, kill with an arrow

Tuingno:ái, tuing enái, kedeái, shoot with bow, hit the mark

Tukạ, nest of bird, a small house

Ṭukui:, earthen pot, jar, jug

Tukup,, tukubo:ái, tukup,, enái, become old and feeble, be decrepit ?

Ṭuku ṭukui ái, ṭuku kedái, cook in haste in a small pot

Tulá,° scales for weighing

Tuliáu:ái, tuliáu enái, kedeái, increase (in wealth, &c.), grow (rich, &c.), fill, rise

Tullạm káskom, cotton

Túlo: á, túl ená, kedái, take up, raise

Tulpái ái, tulpạ ená, kedái, cut the hair straight at the bottom, clip, sport

Tului:, with, in company with,

Tului: chaláu, accompany

Tulujo: á, tului: ená, kedeái, be connected with, compare

Tumál ái, kedái, glean

Tumbudo:ái, tumbut,, enái, kedeái, fall forward, tumble, stumble, fall upon, hang the head through shame

Tumdá:, drum

Tumdá: rui, beat drum

Ṭumkí, small round basket

Tumul, marrow

Ṭunḍango:ái, ṭunḍang enái, walk along (metaphorically used for "life")

Ṭunḍí, yoke (of harness)

Ṭungáu: á, ṭungáu ená, kedái, convey, reach to [bow

Ṭuniáu ái, kedái, fit arrow on

Tunkhi ái, kedái, take care of remember, look after

Tunum baṛái, grope, feel about in the dark

Tunumo:ái, tunum enái, kedeái, feel, handle

Ṭuprí,° cap, hat, crown

Tupuingno: ále, tupuing enále, fight with bows and arrows (see *tuingno:*)

Tupujo:ái, tupui: ená, kedeái, bow down, bend, lodge as grain

Ṭupulá, small basket

Tuṛí, mustard, "*sarsoṇ*"

Tursi,° the sacred tree of the Hindoos

Tursi pindá,° the tulsi shrine of the Hindoos

Tursi jol,° sprinkle water (originally with the tulsi tree)

Turuk, the Mussulmans

Turú tuká, litter, grass or dirt about the house

Ṭuṭi, arrow-head (blunt)

Ṭuṭi eái, kedeái, kill with an arrow, shoot with gun

Tutiya, mouse

Tutkuṛiyạ, hut

Ṭuṭkut,", firebrand, piece of firewood

Ṭuṭuri, to veil the face, cover head

Tuwángo:ái, tuwáng enái, kekeái, rub to pieces,? become very tired or weak from work, wear out

U

Ublạ dublạ, waste, extravagance

Ubo: á, ub ená, kedái, pour out, spill

Uchạro: á, uchạr ená, kedeái, be infectious, remove from place to place

Uchhan,° publish, make known, spread news

Uchhláu: á, uchhláu ená, kedeái,° throw up, cast, vomit

Uchit,† fit, proper

Uchung, jerk, nudge with elbow

Udái pudái ái, kedái, be reduced in circumstances, sink in life, be ruined, spend, waste, throw away uselessly

Udáṇw, report, rumour, fame

Uḍáu:á, uḍáu enái, kedeái,[o] fly

Udgár, hot, warm

Udgár jokhái, summer, hot season

Udhaṛ em,[o] to give on credit

Udo:á, ut„ ená, kedeái, swallow

Udugo: á, udu: kedái, ádeái, direct, guide, show, point out, publish, make known

Udu: káṭup, fore-finger

Uḍui: dubujo:ái, dubui: enái, kedeái, splash in water as a drowning person

Udrí, dropsy, measles

Uḍungre, outside

Uḍung agui, bring out

Uḍung giḍi, throw out

Uḍungo:ái, uḍung ená, kedeái, put out, expel

Udur ái, kedái, grasp,? snore, strangle

Uduṛ dhumá, stout

Uduṛ dhupuṛ, urgently, briskly (a word used chiefly for a person dancing violently)

Uhu, alas!

Uihár ái, kedeái, ponder, remember, consider, grieve

Ujáṛo: á, ujáṛ ená, kedeái,[o] destroy, forsake, be devoured, ruin, desolate

Ujo:ái, ui: enái, kedeái, leap for joy, be moved, excited, stirred up

Ukbukáu:ái, bukáu enái, kedeái, be strangled, suffocated

Ukhráu:á, ukhráu ená, kedái, impress, imprint

Ukhṛí, ukhuṛ,[o] mortar to clean rice

Ukíl,[o] advocate, mediator

Úl, mango

Ulaṭ pulaṭo: á, pulaṭ ená, kedeái,[o] turn upside down, put in confusion, roll from side to side

Ulṭá ulṭí: á, ulṭí ená, kedeái,[o] turn upside down, toss about

Ulṭáu: á, ulṭáu ená, kedeái,[o] upset, move string of tongue as Sántál women do to their newly-born children

Umdhí, deep sleep, trance

Ummadhá: á, ummadhái enái, ummadhá kedeái, prevent, hinder, stop another speaking, stop oxen in ploughing, prevent by an order

Umo:ái, um enái, kedeái, bathe, wash

Umukte, by means of

Umúl, shade, shadow, spirit of the dead

Umúlo: á, umúl enái, kedeái, hide, conceal, shelter

Unhabi:, till then

Unjokhe:, then

Unkhángi, on which [time

Unkhon, thence, from that

Unre, then

Uni, he, that person

Unṭ,† camel

Unumo: á, unum enái, kedeái, sink, be immersed

Úp, hair, wool

Úp áni:, hairy

Upai,† expedient, plan, remedy

Upál bahá,* a kind of white lily

Upạro:ái, upạr enái, kedeái, stir up, excite, help

Upạrre,° concerning

Upạs ái, kedái,° fast, be hungry

Uphlá uphlí: á, uphlí ená, kedeái, rise and fall

Upláu: á, upláu ená, kedeái, emerge from water

Upi muiṇ, ant with wings

Úr, slough (of a snake), skin, rind,? peel?

Úro:ái, úr enái, kedeái, cast the skin, be flayed, loose nail, peel, shell

Urạlo:ái, urạl enái, kedeái, imitate, copy, emulate, feel desire from seeing another's success

Uṛan, to eat (as caterpillars)

Urgam, warm

Uṛi:, a small blackbird

Uṛiáu eái, kedeái, punish

Urihon, a little animal scarcely bigger than a rat

Urijo: á, urí: ená, kedeái, make sure, make fast, tighten

Urláu: á, urláu ená, kedái, pick out, rub and take out what comes to the top (pick out the straws from *dhán*)

Urmál, small bells worn on wrist or ankles

Urú, big black flying beetle

Urudo: á, urut„ ená, kedái, churn, scrape, rub

Urung bhusum, dirty, covered with mud or dust

Uṛut„ uṛut„, expectant, greedy, impatient, surprised

Usạdo:ái, usạt„ enái, kedeái, take offence, be sullen, be grieved, annoyed

Usạrái ái, usạrá kedái, be brisk, actively perform, nimble, strong, active

Usáro: á, usár ená, kedái, widen, wide

Usij ái, usi: kedái, hiss (as a snake)

Uskáu:ái, uskáu enái, kedeái,[o] stir up, excite, raise, lift up, help

Uskup,, uskubo:ái, uskup,, enái, kedeái, turn round in bed, prepare to rise, move just before awaking

Uskur ái, kedái,[o] aggravate, exaggerate, make complaints, put wood on fire

Usul ái, kedái,[o] pay, settle a debt

Usúl, high, tall

Usúlo:ái, usúl enái, kedeái, be tall or high

Uṭái ái, uṭa kedái, root as a pig

Uṭar, some, &c. (answering to "*sá*" in Hindustáni), many

Uṭháu: ái, uṭháu ená, kedeái, shut up (as a shop), part, go away, leave, depart

Uṭháu chabái, be abolished

Uṭhkáu idí, take away, take off

Uṭhulá, top of fireplace, stones placed round the cooking-hole

Uṭi, joint of body

Utingno: á, uting ená, kedái, barter, exchange one thing for another

Uṭkáu: á, uṭkáu ená, kedeái, exhume, remove, dig out, root out from bottom

Utpátáu:ái, utpátáu enái, be mischievous,? be solicitous, eager, anxious, determined, resolved

Utú, seasoning (vegetables, fish, &c.)

Y

Yih,? this

Yih ái, kedeái, do this, do so

Z

Zámino: ái, zámin enái, kedeái,† become bail